# Mustang
## 5.0 & 4.6
### 1979 – 1998

**Matt Stone**

MBI Publishing Company

First published in 1998 by MBI Publishing Company, 729 Prospect Avenue, PO Box 1, Osceola, WI 54020-0001 USA.

MBI Publishing Company books are also available at discounts in bulk quantity for industrial or sales-promotional use. For details write to Special Sales Manager at the Motorbooks International Wholesalers & Distributors, 729 Prospect Avenue, PO Box 1, Osceola, WI 54020-0001 USA.

Library of Congress Cataloging-in-Publication Data

Stone, Matt.
    Mustang 5.0 and 4.6: 1979-1998/ Matt Stone.
            p. cm. -- (Muscle car color history)
    Includes index.
    ISBN 0-7603-0334-7 (pbk. : alk. paper)
    1. Mustang automobile--History. 2. Mustang automobile--Pictorial works. I. Title. II. Series.
    TL215.M8S695    1998
    629.222'2--dc21                    97-46055

**On the front cover:** Ford's 1996 SVT Cobra convertible and 1991 Mustang LX represent the two generations, and two most popular bodystyles, of the late-model Mustang. *Matt Stone*

**On the frontispiece:** Ford appended the HO to its 5.0-liter V-8 in 1982 launching what the faithful consider the beginning of the new Mustang performance era. This cast plate graced 1987-1993 5.0-liter V-8s. *Matt Stone*

**On the title page:** A pair of 1998 Mustang Cobras, coupe and convertible. These cars offer some of the best performance-for-the-dollar fun available. *Ford Special Vehicle Team*

**On the back cover:** Top: 5.0-liter Mustangs make potent competitors at numerous racing venues, most notably Trans-Am and drag racing. *SUPER FORD* Bottom: Strong ties to its pony-car predecessors was a major goal of the design and marketing teams which worked on the 1994 Mustang. *Ford Motor Company publicity photo*

All Ford sales brochure, print ad, and press release photos used with permission of Ford Motor Company.

Edited by Zack Miller
Designed by Katie L. Sonmor

Printed in Hong Kong through World Print, Ltd.

# Dedication

This book is dedicated to the memory of the late Len Frank who helped me get started in this business that I love so much, to the membership of the Motor Press Guild, and to my mom and dad who not only put up with, but nurtured, my habits as a car fool.

# contents

# Acknowledgments

A project like this can't happen in a vacuum. I had more help than I can believe in putting this book together. *In no particular order*, my thanks to:

Ford SVT Public Relations: Jim Sawyer, John Clor, Dan Reid, Cathy Weber, Julie Kalbfleisch, and Alan Hall.

Ford Public Affairs in California: John Clinard, Harold Allen, Bill George, Linda Hainley, and the Royal Automotive Fleet goddess, Sandra Badgett.

Ford Public Affairs in Detroit: Mike Moran, Dan Bedore, Whitney Said, and especially, Sarah Perris, who diligently coordinated many interviews with several Ford executives.

My buds at *SUPER FORD* magazine: Tom Wilson, Steve Turner, and Mary Jean Wesche.

Steve and Liz Saleen, Jimmy Moore, Melissa Denoff, and everyone at Saleen Performance.

Fellow professionals in the automotive media business who contributed their efforts and talents: Scott Mead, David W. Newhardt, E. John Thawley III and especially Patrick C. Paternie who greatly assisted by authoring chapter 9.

Tim Boyd, Ford Special Vehicles marketing manager.

John Coletti, Manager, Special Vehicle Engineering.

Janine Bay, Mustang Chief Project Engineer.

Jim Clarke, Chief Engineer, Advanced and Preprogram Powertrain Engineering.

Lee Hamkins, Special Vehicle Operations.

Jack Witucki, Mustang-Thunderbird Brand Manager.

Bob Bondurant.

Tommy Kendall.

Kim Seguin, JMPR.

Zack Miller, senior editor; Katie L. Sonmor, senior designer; and Tim Parker, president, of Motorbooks International.

Art Gould.

Max Jones, Lina Vitale, and Joe Thompson, Roush Racing and Roush Industries.

Gretchen M. Jacobs, California Highway Patrol.

Ron and crew at Bill Stroppe & Son, who ably handle Ford's press fleet.

Mike, Jean, and Jeff O'Brien, and staff at Flags Photo Center.

The automotive aftermarket, which has a great influence on making the Mustang as popular as it is, with a special thanks to those companies that sent in materials for the aftermarket section of this book.

My family: Linda, Melissa, Maureen, Mom, Dad, other Mom, and all the sisters and brothers, nieces, nephews, and dogs.

A special thanks to those whose cars appear in the photographs contained herein, whether by design, or just by being "snapped" along the way.

Lastly, my thanks to *you*, for digging into your pocket and pulling out your hard-earned cash (or well-seasoned credit card) and buying this book. If you didn't, I'd have had no reason for writing it.

—Matt Stone

# Introduction

To many people, the Ford Mustang means a red 1966 convertible, pony interiors, the Shelby GT 350. It means 289 Hi-Po V-8s, the Boss 302, or the Mach 1. Mustang may bring to mind names like Lee Iacocca, Carroll Shelby, or maybe your uncle or aunt who bought a new Mustang some 30 years ago. Mustang does indeed mean all of this and more.

But to a different generation of enthusiasts, Mustang means something else: 5.0-liter engines, five-speed transmissions, 70-mm throttle bodies, SVT Cobras. Fox and SN-95. Saleen, Steeda, and an SVO catalog. The new Mustangs.

The tales and details of how the original Mustang came to be are worthy ones, but they've been well told, many times over. Had it not happened there would be no new Mustangs; that's for sure. By the same token, most Mustang history books drop the curtain with the 1973 models, the last of the so-called "classic era" Mustangs. But the story doesn't end there (although it almost did).

Mustang enthusiasm suffered through the mid-1970s, a time when performance motoring just about died altogether. Fuel shortages, stringent bumper and emission requirements, and public antipathy took their toll. And the Mustang wasn't the only victim: Chevrolet dropped the Camaro Z-28 at the end of the 1974 model year. For Mustang, 1974 marked the segue from the larger-than-ever 1973s to a new Pinto-based car, the Mustang II. Tough times they were.

But then something happened. A new Mustang came along in 1979 that demonstrated that the nameplate had life and Ford had brains. Then a new GT for 1982, 225 horsepower for 1987, a redesign in 1994, Cobras and 305 horsepower, and the Mustang was back in business. It is this era and these Mustangs that this book is about. Though I'll touch on Turbo Cobras, the SVOs, and the Mercury Capri version, Mustang's key to performance has always been a thumping V-8 engine of one sort or another, hence the title of this book.

Mustang life, as many of today's younger enthusiasts know it, began again in 1979 and fortunately, continues to this day. An entire aftermarket industry is built around the 1979–1993 Mustangs, and early returns indicate the 1994-to-current version is picking up where the last of those original Fox-bodied cars left off. For all the racing success garnered by Shelby Mustangs and Boss 302s, the trophies taken home by modern-era Mustangs are just as significant and even more in number. A full chapter is dedicated to these track-bound champs.

Lest you think I have only viewed from afar, I'm pleased to say I owned a black-over-gray-leather, 1991 5.0-liter LX fastback from the day it was new in January 1991 until August 1997, when this book was well underway. It always looked great, ran great, and went like stink, with nary a problem in the almost 80,000 miles I drove it.

There have been challenges to the Mustang's success and to its survival. Buyers' needs and tastes are forever changing, so there will certainly be more. For now, however, Mustang remains. It remains the original American sporty-performance coupe, very much true to its original form, and it continues to be the best-selling nameplate of the breed some 30 years hence. So ride on, ye pony.

# *one* An All New

# Mustang
## 1979-1981

As we all know, the 1964-1/2 Ford Mustang was an automotive "shot heard 'round the world." But in an all-too-brief decade, times had changed. Instead of a horsepower war, we had 5-mile-per-hour bumpers. Instead of cheap gas, we had the Arab Oil Embargo. And when it came time to introduce a new Mustang for 1974, we got a chrome-plated Pinto.

Now Mustang II fans will assuredly be quick to defend it, but the fact of the matter was clear. In just five years, we went from Boss 302s and 429s, to your choice of a 2.3-liter, four-cylinder engine or a 2.8-liter V-6. There were no more Shelby Mustangs; instead we had the tepid Mustang II, with a vinyl top, fake wire wheelcovers, and whitewall tires. Yes, there was a Mach 1 version, but anyone could see it was but a mere shadow of its former self.

In Ford's defense, the mid-1970s could hardly be called the heyday of automotive performance. Ferrari struggled to sell its final Daytonas, and Jaguar did the same with the last of the thirsty 1974 V-12 E-Types. Camaro Z-28 sales were so dismal for 1974 that the model was unceremoniously dropped from the 1975 line-up. Though Pontiac still offered a Trans-Am that year, its emasculated 400-cubic-inch V-8 couldn't even muster 200 horsepower. Automakers were having a miserable time dealing with the new emission, safety, and fuel-economy regulations, so technological resources and budgets

Mustang had been offered in fastback and notchback form from 1965 through 1978 and as a convertible from 1965 through 1973. Ford stuck with the fastback and notchback formula for the 1979 models. Though a bit less sporty than the fastback, the upright notchback actually possessed greater chassis stability. Though this particular car was a four-cylinder base model, it was equipped with the TRX suspension, wheels, and tires. *Ford Motor Company*

Early concept drawing for what would become the new-for-1979 Ford Mustang and Mercury Capri. The square headlights are already in place, and the blockish grille shapes are similar to the final Capri design. A part of the lower-air dam area resembles that same feature on the 1992 Camaro. This rendering is dated January 1977. *Ford Motor Company*

were absorbed making the cars meet the new specs, not increasing their performance.

Another issue was the social factors present at the time. The aforementioned gas shortage drove fuel prices to all-time highs, so big V-8s became unfashionable in an equally big hurry. The American economy was still suffering the effects of Watergate and a recession, so car sales were down in general. And the environmental movement focused its sights on the automobile as one of the forces bent on destroying the earth and its natural resources. Right or wrong, it was a tough climate for fast cars.

Ford did its best to invigorate Mustang enthusiasm with the Pinto-derived Mustang II, but it landed with a dull thud in spite of good initial sales. Although Lee Iacocca was seemingly on every magazine cover when the original Mustang was introduced, when Ford tried

At least the Mustang II finished a bit stronger than it started. V-8 power returned for 1975, and in order to keep its arms around the Cobra name (for which it had wrestled with Carroll Shelby), the company applied it to the Mustang II model beginning in 1976 (1978-model shown). In Ford's defense, it did the best it could with what it had at the time, giving the Cobra II a V-8 engine, a four-speed manual transmission, power disc brakes, a rear stabilizer bar, heavy-duty springs, and alloy wheels. Still, it was largely a "paint and tape" performance package with none of the performance potential of the Mustangs of just a few years before. *Ford Motor Company publicity photo*

to recreate the same marketing magic 10 years later, the walk didn't match the talk.

The hardware actually improved a bit during the Mustang II's five-year run. A 302 V-8 option returned for 1975, the first year that most manufacturers had to resort to the catalytic converter as a means of meeting the no-lead gas emissions requirements. It was rated at—fasten your seatbelts—122 horsepower. Bigger news for some was the "Silver Luxury Group" package, replete with a silver half-top and Cranberry velour interior. Mustang sales responded . . . by dropping more than 50 percent from the 1974 figures.

At least someone was trying in 1976, as the V-8 engine was re-calibrated to deliver 139 horsepower, and the Cobra II package debuted. With its blue-stripes-on-white color combination, wings, and spoilers, it attempted to recall the Shelby Mustangs of just a decade prior. But it was all cosmetic; not a single hardware improvement was part of the deal.

The strategy for 1977, a carryover year, was to use appearance-minded "tape and paint" packages in an attempt to carry the day for performance. The V-8 continued to be a popular option, even in California, where it could only be had with a three-speed automatic; buyers from "the other 49" could at least get a four-speed stick.

In retrospect, 1978 was historically significant to Mustang for at least three reasons. First, it was the final year for the Mustang II. Sales for the five-year run were exceptional, especially compared to some previous and several later versions. From a sales perspective, Ford's management and stockholders viewed the car as a reasonable success. Secondly, a new Mustang debuted in 1979 (much more on that as we go). And finally, it was the year Iacocca, Father of the Mustang and auto executive par excellence, was unceremoniously fired by chairman Henry Ford II. He joined Chrysler shortly thereafter.

"The Way We Were" . . . and it wasn't all good. In the press release that accompanied this 1974 press photo, Ford declared the "new Mustang II combines value and economy while maintaining its sport heritage." Few enthusiasts would agree that its vinyl top, ample chrome trim, and whitewall tires recall much of the Mustang GTs, Shelby GT 350s, and Boss 302s of the previous decade, especially with the new Mustang II being mostly Pinto underneath the skin. *Ford Motor Company publicity photo*

The big news, as it was, for 1978 was the King Cobra model. Besides a raft of add-on plastic flares, scoops, and spoilers, the King Cobra attempted to pack some improved hardware. It was available only with the V-8 and was packaged with a rear anti-sway bar, heavy-duty shocks, increased cooling capacity, and the best 13-inch wheels and tires Goodyear could muster. It was no Boss 302, but it was an admirable improvement for a last-year effort.

Ford Mustang or Fiat X1/9? This March 1976 in-house rendering shows a possible Mustang in the form of a notchback coupe with an exceptionally low beltline and hideaway headlights. Look at the actual 1979 car, and you won't see too much of this concept remaining. *Ford Motor Company*

The new-for-1979 Ford Mustang Cobra under hard cornering. Notice lift of right front tire and squat at the back caused by acceleration. This car was a Turbo model, the performance offering of choice for 1979. The hood scoop was nonfunctional and the snake graphic less than tasteful. Hood graphics worked for the Firebird, so Ford gave it a try. Note that all the bodywork below the perimeter rub-strip was painted black, which made the tallish Fox platform look a bit sleeker. *Ford Motor Company*

It turns out the 1979 Mustang was already nearing the drawing board about the time the Mustang II came out. As mentioned, the gas crunch rocked the nation and its auto makers, impressing upon them that lighter, more fuel-efficient car designs would be important in the coming decade. The federal government's Corporate Average Fuel Economy (CAFE), which came along about the same time, underscored this need to any others that may have missed the point. CAFE was to become a requirement beginning in 1978, and the minimum average-fuel-mileage of a manufacturer's fleet had to increase on a sliding scale until it reached 27.5 miles per gallon for the 1985 models. There were a million loopholes, but it was clear a Boss 429 would not be slipping through any of them.

Ford began work on its "Fox" platform of cars in mid-1973; the first results were the Ford Fairmont/Mercury Zephyr line of coupes and sedans. These mainstream cars were hailed as among the first American mid-size models designed around European themes: sharper handling, space and fuel efficient, cost-effective cars built to economically satisfy the transportation needs of middle America. One magazine categorized the Fairmont sedan as a "firmed up Volvo," not exactly exciting, but purposeful. The Fairmont/Zephyr came to market in 1978, the same year the CAFE requirements took effect.

Shortly after Fox platform development was underway, Ford decided it would serve as the foundation for the next-generation Mustang. Many automotive visionaries have long dreamed of creating "the world car." It would be a versatile, universal platform that could be tailored for dozens, even hundreds, of worldwide automotive

markets with a minimum of expense. The concept centers around economies of scale, the amortization of development costs. There was a movement at Ford, headed by product whiz Hal Sperlich, to make the Fox that international platform—the do-all for many markets. But it was an idea whose time had not yet come, at least in terms of an American-designed product that would be manufactured in, and adequately appeal to, the other markets. Among other reasons, regulatory issues and production methods kept the Fox at home. Ultimately, this philosophy was played out with both the Ford Escort of 1981 and, to an even greater degree, the Mondeo/Contour of the early 1990s. Furthermore, "world platforming" has become the basis of a recent reorganizational and operational plan called Ford 2000, which will set the tone for the company's processes, designs, and operations into the new millennium.

Ford's Product Planning and Research department turned the Fox project over to North American Automotive Operations in mid-1975. The goal was to develop it into both Ford and Mercury sedan variants, as well as the new Mustang. Although corporate planning no longer required it to be a world-car platform, the original plans included yielding an all-new Pinto. But because it appeared the Pinto would be replaced by the Escort, the Pinto was removed from the Fox chassis development program early on. The Pinto vanished after the 1980 model year, replaced by the front-wheel-drive Escort in 1981.

There *was* a world car that *did* get folded into the Fox program. It was the Capri, designed and built by Ford of Europe, and it sold in numerous world markets. When the German-built Capri hit our shores in 1971, it was sold through Lincoln-Mercury, which was becoming

# 1979 Mustang Indy Pace Car

Few automotive events cast a glow as bright as the Indianapolis 500. Though the Speedway and its promoters have known all manner of success and turmoil over the Brickyard's nearly 90-year history, several elements of its aura have remained constant: the singing of "Back Home Again in Indiana," the drinking of milk in the winner's circle, and big promotional value to the automaker that gets to pace "The Greatest Spectacle in Racing."

Pacing the 1964 Indy 500 helped launch the original Mustang. Hoping that some of the original Mustang's good luck would rub off on the new Fox car in 1979, Ford successfully vied to pace the race again.

In order to meet Indy's requirements of sustained 125-mile-an-hour running, Ford went to one of its usual sources when it came to special performance development: Jack Roush. At the time Roush had attained genius status as an engine builder, and he was put in charge of developing the cars.

There were two interesting twists to the project. One was that even though Michelin was Ford's performance tire of choice, the actual pace cars had to run Goodyear tires. This was due to the Speedway's contractual obligations to the tire maker. The second odd bit was that Ford chose to develop V-8-powered pace cars . . . even though it was purporting the turbocharged four to be the performance way of the future. As the blown four was a new animal at the time, it was probably a case of "going with what you know."

Roush and his team built 302 engines loaded with heavy-duty racing or Boss 302 parts. The hardware included forged cranks, four-barrel carbs, aluminum intake manifolds, 351 Windsor heads, and free-flow dual-exhaust systems. They were good for 250 to 260 horsepower, more than enough to pace the field and be completely reliable. These V-8s, which would have been just the ticket for the production Mustang, were backed by uprated Ford C-4 three-speed automatic transmissions and extra-tall rear-end ratios to allow easy high-speed running.

The chassis required very little upgrading, and the two cars actually used to pace the race were T-top configuration (not offered until 1981 on production models). The whole package was finished off in a light metallic beige color scheme, with black, orange, and dark red striping, plus the usual Indianapolis Motor Speedway identification. The interior employed special Recaro seats and the switchgear for the lighting and communications gear required of a pace car.

Prior to the 1970s, a manufacturer just built the pace cars, took the PR photos, and left it at that. Then it became fashionable to produce commemorative "pace car editions" to further capitalize on the honor of leading the field of 33 toward the green flag. Ford produced about 11,000 Indy Pace Car Mustangs. They wore the same colors and stripes as did the real pace cars and could be had with either the 5.0-liter V-8 or turbo-four driveline. The Recaro seats were also offered, though the pace car Mustangs were available in hatchback form only, sans the special T-roof arrangement.

A pace car failing to perform in front of the world's TV audience would be embarrassing, but Ford suffered none of that. The cars performed flawlessly, pacing a young sophomore driver named Rick Mears to what would be his first of four Indy victories. It had been 15 years since the Mustang paced the 500, and it would be another 15 years before it would happen again.

The new-for-1979 Mustang interior was offered in base, sport, and Ghia levels of trim, with several different optional accent packages. Leather seating surfaces were something new. This factory catalog photo shows the top-line Ghia interior with leather trim. This car had power door locks but not power windows. At least the emergency brake handle was on the console, not on the floor. *Ford Motor Company*

Ford's "captive import" division. L-M was also handling the DeTomaso Pantera mid-engined exotic. The Capri was billed as "The Sexy European," and the name fit well. A taut sports coupe with precise rack and pinion steering, crisp Euro-styling, and a willing 2.0-liter overhead-cam (OHC) four, the Capri was enjoyable to drive and a solid seller for L-M. Together, Capri and Pantera probably dropped the average age of people visiting an L-M dealer by at least 20 years.

When the Capri came out with a 2.6-liter, German-built V-6 in 1972, it appealed to American buyers who wanted some power and sporty handling. This 60-degree, "Cologne" V-6 would be stretched to 2.8-liters for the 1974 Capri and was the same V-6 used in the Mustang II, though the Capri was a more satisfying car to drive. A revised Capri II came out in mid-1975, retaining the basic flavor of the original Capri but offering a bit more room, comfort, and storage capacity by virtue of its hatchback design.

So, just as Mercury would get a Zephyr version of the Fox platform sedans, Ford decided the division should have a piece of the new Mustang as well. *Road & Track's* John Dinkel wrote ". . . the Capri has fallen on hard times, initially from dollar/deutsche mark parity problems coupled with difficulty in keeping a designed-in-Europe car up to date with respect to U.S. legislation and more recently from increased competition, especially

of the Japanese variety. The handwriting was on the wall, and Ford decided not to import any 1978 Capri IIs, preferring instead to sell off the remaining 1977 models in preparation for the launch of the all-new 1979 domestic Capri." So after thoughts of world cars and new Pintos fell by the wayside, the die was cast for the Fox platform: Fairmont and Zephyr two-door coupes and two- and four-door sedans for 1978 and a new Ford Mustang and Mercury Capri for 1979.

Fox was the recipient of more computer-aided design and wind-tunnel testing than any previous Ford program. Weight reduction was emphasized. It was simple enough: If power from the new "emissions" engines was down and better fuel economy was required, less weight would yield improved performance and gas mileage. Unit-body construction was employed. The sedans were built on a 105.5-inch wheelbase, and the Mustang-Capri sport coupes were 100.4 inches.

The front suspension was a modified MacPherson strut design, using coil springs instead of the oft-employed torsion bars; a solid axle with a four-link suspension layout was used in the rear end. Anti-sway bars were utilized front and rear on all models, varying in diameter and stiffness depending upon which car and engine package was specified. Rack and pinion steering was standard, already recognized for its greater precision and road feel than the old recirculating ball designs. A key to the platform's success was its ability to work with all manner of drivelines: four-cylinders, V-6s, straight sixes, V-8s, and automatic and manual transmissions. The Fairmont-Zephyr and Mustang-Capri offered all of these options.

The Fox platform was primarily designed to yield sedans. The shapes for the Fairmont-Zephyr came together easily. Unfortunately, the sedan's "hard-points"—design parameters and basic measurements that supposedly cannot be changed—yielded looks that were a bit too blockish for the sport coupes. With an image car like Mustang, styling was a critical element to the car's success—or failure. Enter Jack Telnack, a long-time Ford executive who had just completed a stint in Europe. He was executive director for Ford's North American Light Car and Truck Design in 1976 when the Mustang and Capri were being styled.

According to Telnack, "We took some liberties in the interest of improved aerodynamics. One of the basic themes for this car was 'form follows function' and we wanted to be as aerodynamically correct as possible before getting into the wind tunnel. . . . With the Mustang-Capri, the designers were thinking about aerodynamics in the initial sketch stages, which made the tuning job in the tunnel much easier."

Nobody could complain that the new Mustang and Capri didn't offer something for everyone with a total of four engine choices between the two cars. Three of these are pictured here, from left: the 2.8-liter V-6, the newly developed 140-horsepower, turbocharged four-cylinder in the middle, and the old standby 302 V-8, which was officially denoted as the 5.0 for the first time. *Ford Motor Company*

One of the adjustments was the height of the cowl. Surprisingly, it was raised by an inch, not lowered as one might suspect. "What kind of designer would raise the cowl on a car?" Telnack asked in an interview with *Road & Track*. "We did it because we wanted to get a faster-sloping hood and we had to pivot the hood over the air cleaner. This allowed us to lower the leading edge of the hood to give the car a slightly wedge-shape profile that produces less drag. Unfortunately, it also required inner front fender aprons and radiator supports different from the comparable Fairmont parts, but we felt the increased fuel economy promised by the slicker design justified the additional investment."

Though completely American, the styling treatment smacked of European influence. As opposed to the ultra-long-hood, short-deck look of their chief competitors, Camaro and Firebird, the Mustang and Capri were considerably more "upright," and had a more open greenhouse. The new cars were hatchbacks, as opposed to the GM twins that were pure coupes. Though not as racy, they were a more efficient package. This was in keeping with Ford's goals and was somewhat dictated by the shared-sedan underpinnings. The Mustang and Capri had more headroom, better visibility, more rear-seat leg room, and more storage capacity. Yet, they were smaller and lighter than their nemesis machines from Pontiac and Chevy. The performance pendulum always swings back and forth between the Ford and GM cars. Some years, Ford had the hot setup; for others, the GM cars could run and hide.

Most agreed the new cars were a substantial styling improvement over the Mustang II. The integrating of the 5-mile-per-hour bumpers was much better. A neat, black rub-strip served as the leading edge of the bumpers and as side-door nick protection. As a styling element, it made the cars seem longer, and it gave the overall design a completeness. Both cars utilized the square headlights that had come into fashion just a few

The Sexy European meets the Original Pony Car. For 1979 Mustang and Capri shared platforms for the first time. The Capri was offered only in hatchback form. The blockish grille, square front hoodline, and IMSA GT-inspired fender flares were the main stylistic differences. In keeping with the European theme, the Capri's engine designations were all metric: 2.3, 2.8, and 5.0. This is a base 2.3 model. *Ford Motor Company*

years earlier. The Mustang implemented an egg-crate grille style, while the Capri had a horizontal-bar theme.

Besides the grille and badging, Ford did a commendable job of trying to separate the appearance of the two cars while staying within budget and design parameters. The rear spoilers on performance models of the Mustang and Capri were different, as were the "gills" just aft of the rear side windows. The main sheet metal distinction was the way the fender-flare treatments were handled. The Mustang's were a conventional arching flare that followed the shape of the wheelwell, while the Capri got a "blister" flare, apparently styled after the International Motorsports Association racers of the day. This "cafe racer" touch made the Capri look a bit wider and more substantial. Considering that the Fox Mustang would ultimately outlive the Capri by several model years and receive wider tire and wheel packages, perhaps it should have been the other way around.

The Mustang was offered in two body styles: hatchback and two-door sedan (notchback) with a standard trunk. The Capri was available only as a hatchback. No convertible model was developed for the 1979 introduction of the new cars.

The following chart demonstrates how the new Mustang and Capri base models stacked up against their predecessors and competitors:

|  | 1979 Mustang/ Capri | 1978 Mustang II | 1977 Capri II |
|---|---|---|---|
| Wheelbase (in) | 100.4 | 96.2 | 100.9 |
| Length (in) | 179.1 | 175.0 | 174.8 |
| Width (in) | 67.4 | 70.2 | 64.8 |
| Height (in) | 51.6 | 50.3 | 51.0 |
| Curb weight (lbs) | 2,520 | 2,710 | 2,590 |

|  | Toyota Celica | Chevrolet Monza | Pontiac Firebird |
|---|---|---|---|
| Wheelbase (in) | 98.4 | 97.0 | 108.0 |
| Length (in) | 173.6 | 179.3 | 197.8 |
| Width (in) | 64.4 | 65.4 | 74.5 |
| Height (in) | 51.6 | 50.2 | 49.2 |
| Curb weight (lbs) | 2,505 | 2,760 | 3,400 |

This chart reveals several identifiable trends. First of all, Ford was successful with its goals of weight reduction, though this weight was for a base four-cylinder car; loaded V-8 cars were much heavier. In spite of the fact that the new Mustang was 4 inches longer in wheelbase and overall length than the Mustang II, it weighed around 200 pounds less (depending upon model and equipment). It also was considerably more weight/space efficient than the Camaro, a design that dated back to mid-1970. The Mustang was also longer, lower, and wider than the Camaro. At the same time, the Mustang-Capri platform offered a bit more size than most of its foreign competition, such as the Celica, the Scirocco, or Nissan's 200 SX.

The original Mustang had great appeal—and notched impressive sales—because it could be tailored to be many things to many people. Grandma felt comfortable in the six-cylinder automatic notchback, and Carroll Shelby could make a race car out of the 289 Hi-Po four-speed fastback. Ford was smart enough to recognize this in the development of the Fox-bodied cars and offered an exceptionally wide array of powerplants.

The base engine was the 2.3-liter, single-overhead-cam (SOHC), four-cylinder Lima engine (so called because it was built at Ford's Lima, Ohio, plant) that debuted in the Pinto and Mustang II of 1974. It could be ordered with a four-speed manual transmission or a three-speed automatic. Rated at 88 horsepower, it was the ideal choice for rental cars, teenaged drivers, and commuters. For performance there were other choices.

Next up was the same 2.8-liter German V-6 that served well in the Capri II. It was smooth and reasonably torquey. It was a smart mid-level powerplant offering, despite the mandatory three-speed automatic transmission. Given its rev-happy nature, the V-6 car fairly cried out for a manual transmission. Keep in mind, however, that manufacturers had to invest considerable sums to "certify" each driveline offering for emissions and fuel-economy compliance. As Ford had two other performance offerings planned, it had to keep an eye on the costs of offering too many variations. The V-6 was offered in the Capri only for 1979. An old Ford standby, the 200-cubic-inch straight six was available in the Mustang. It was dependable and put to best use in rental car fleets.

Ford learned a lesson about Mustangs in 1974: Always have a V-8 available. When the 1979 Mustang was being planned, two performance-oriented offerings were in place. One was the tried-and-true 302, which could be mated with either a four-speed manual

The Michelin TRX wheel/tire/suspension package was the first use of a metric-spec wheel and tire and the first time a wheel and tire were designed to work as a system on a mass-produced car. The wheels were a bit taller than the most aggressive 15-inch applications of the day, and the tires gave ride and handling that was better than anything else Ford offered at the time. As the Mustang got heavier and more powerful, the TRX tires got larger to accommodate the increase in grip required. BMW and Ferrari adopted use of the TRX system until tire and wheel manufacturers began offering products in the more common 16-inch configuration. *Scott Mead*

transmission or three-speed automatic (auto only in California). It was rated at 140 horsepower. The 302 designation, however, was chucked and the engine was officially referred to as the 5.0-liter V-8. Ford was thinking performance again, and the 5.0 chrome badge on the flanks of the 1979 Mustang served notice on the streets.

In the mid-1970s, turbocharging was the performance enhancer of choice for many manufacturers. The theory was simple enough: Make a small engine perform like a big one on demand. When trundling around town or cruising on the freeway at light throttle openings, small turbocharged engines would be "off boost" and offer good gas mileage. Get into the gas pedal, and the exhaust-driven turbo would boost the power to levels that were previously attainable only by the larger engines. In the history of the automobile, there have been many turbocharged cars, but the first modern application came from Porsche in 1976. The Buick Regal was the first modern American car to venture into turbo designs with a 3.8-liter V-6 in 1979. That same year Ford offered a turbocharged Mustang Cobra.

Ford engineers started out with the 2.3-liter four, and added a Garrett AiResearch TO-3 turbocharger altered to Ford specifications—a modified intake manifold and an electronic retard device that reacted to turbo boost to avoid, or minimize, detonation. The performance increase was substantial, but durability became a problem. To combat the deficiencies, the engine was bolstered with forged pistons and redesigned piston rings. To provide adequate turbo lubrication, oil pressure was boosted and sump capacity was increased by a 1/2 quart. Both intake and exhaust valves were upgraded with sodium-filled units helping dissipate heat on the exhaust side. The engine continued with two-barrel carburetion, though carburetors were not particularly well suited to turbocharged engines (as both Ford and Buick would later learn). Fuel injection would later prove the way to better driveability and increased performance.

The turbo-four was rated at 132 horsepower, 8 horsepower less than the 5.0-liter V-8. All turbocharged cars had the four-speed manual transmission. In an attempt to retain some low-end torque (often a problem in small-displacement turbo applications), the engine maintained its 9.0:1 compression ratio and ran a relatively conservative 6 pounds of boost. This application was a "draw through" design instead of a "blow through" layout (pressurized carburetor), as was the original Paxton-blown Shelby Mustangs. Norm General, assistant chief engineer for the program, said at the time, "Early in the development program we dropped compression to 7.2:1 in conjunction with 9 to 11 psi-boost and got about the same wide-open-throttle performance, but part-throttle performance was quite dead. This system we've chosen retains reasonable part-throttle performance and gets the high end."

The underpinnings of the new Mustang and Capri were considerably better than the Pinto-derived components of their predecessors: struts up front, a four-link located live axle out back, and coil springs at all four corners. Three levels of suspension were offered: base, handling, and TRX. The handling upgrade brought stiffer springs, shocks, and bushings, and the TRX option went a step further.

At that time 15-inch wheel and tire packages were as aggressive as you could get. The Mustang II made due with dismal 13-inchers. TRX was a radical new concept, a dedicated wheel and tire system developed and patented by Michelin. The new Mustang and Capri were the first domestic cars to use it. In the European mode, they were designed to "metric spec": the modified three-spoke alloy wheels were 390x150-mm units, equal to 15.4x5.9 inches. This is impressive considering that the Chevrolet Corvette's 16-inch wheels—the most aggressive available at the time—were not introduced until 1984! The aspect ratio measured about 65, a big step forward from the 70- and 75-series of the time.

The goals of TRX were better handling with acceptable ride quality, low rolling-resistance, and high grip-levels. The heightened performance offered by these tires allowed the engineers to tailor the suspension accordingly and specifically for it. The only rub with the package was that it married the customer to Michelin tires; the unique wheel size would not accommodate anything else. But like any good system, if the components can be properly matched, the results could be greater than the sum of the parts.

Interior and exterior packages also followed the three-level formula, with base, Ghia, and Mustang Cobra/Capri RS trim. There were minor variations between the Ford and Mercury, not to mention the tailorability of many stand-alone options. The top performance offering was intended to be the Mustang Cobra option package, which combined the turbo four-cylinder engine, TRX suspension/tire package, and the usual tape/stripe and ID trim.

The completely new interior was a reasonable combination of sport and luxury. Perhaps best of all was a dash layout that resided squarely in front of the driver and offered the option of full instrumentation. This included a plainly visible speedometer and tach, as well as four ancillary gauges: fuel, temperature, oil pressure, and ammeter. There was a glass, flip-up sunroof to compensate for the lack of a convertible. The Cobra version had a black dash fascia instead of the faux wood of the other versions. Overall, the interior was much improved over the Mustang II.

In simple terms, the first turbo-four-powered Mustangs were a valiant effort, but most road testers of the day preferred the V-8. With its low restriction exhaust, it sounded "like a Pantera" according to one scribe, when compared to the buzzy four-banger. With careful options selection, the V-8 could be tailored to be the sleeper performance model of the line-up. Zero-to-60 times—the performance measurement American drivers most appreciated—were in the 8.5-to-8.7-second range for the V-8 cars, while the turbos were lucky to break the 10.0-second barrier. The four was also a bit rough and boomy, and the early cars suffered from driveability problems such as poor hot starting and stumbling when cold. Ford replaced many turbochargers under warranty on the 1979–1981 cars. So much for the first-generation turbo-four as Mustang's performance leader.

If the top-line engine offering wasn't exactly what everyone was hoping for, the TRX rolling stock and suspension system didn't disappoint. The handling of a TRX-equipped Mustang or Capri was miles ahead of the old Mustang II and most everything else the Mustang competed with at the time. Working with the purpose-calibrated shocks, springs, and bushings, the low-profile tires delivered sharper turn-in, and the tread pattern yielded admirable cornering limits. Road tests of the day showed cornering forces consistently between 0.75 g and 0.8 g—as good as the Chevrolet Corvette of the day and better than the Camaro. The only fly in the ointment was excessive wheel-hop, especially in the torquey 5.0 cars.

Though not perfect, the new cars were a success in every sense of the term. They proved to be a well-conceived, and as we know now, long-lived design. The market certainly responded to the new cars; Mustang sales nearly doubled from 192,410 for the last of the Mustang IIs, to 369,936 for 1979.

Things got both better and worse for 1980. The better part came in the form of optional Recaro front seats, as used in the 1979 Indy Pace Car Mustangs (see sidebar). This gave comfort and lateral support to match the Mustang's cornering prowess and hinted that its performance targets included BMWs and not just Camaros.

The worse came in the form of fewer cubic inches and less horsepower. The promising 2.8-liter V-6 option was eliminated, leaving the 3.3-liter straight six as the only mid-level option. The base 2.3 and the turbo 2.3-liter fours carried over basically unchanged, but the worst news was a *downsized* V-8.

The 5.0 (née 302) was reduced in size to 255 cubic inches via a reduction in the cylinder bore from 4.00 to 3.68 inches. Ford needed better mileage from its fleet of engines, and the method to achieve it at the time was fewer cubic inches. Though the 255-cubic-inch displacement was identical to the successful Ford dual-overhead-cam (DOHC) Indy V-8 racing engine, the similarities ended there. Horsepower dropped from 140 to a lowly 119. Other than the V-8-less Mustang II of 1974, this era, lasting from 1980 to 1981, must be considered the low point of Mustang performance.

On the plus side, a new four-speed overdrive transmission was introduced in mid-year. When combined with the V-8, it gave at least some hint of performance orientation, but the numbers certainly didn't back it up. Most of the V-8 cars came with automatics anyway.

For 1981 there was another mixed bag of choices. A new T-roof option provided more of a convertible feeling. A Traction Lok axle helped reduce the annoying wheel-hop problem in the performance-optioned cars. The 255-cubic-inch V-8 was re-rated to 120 horsepower, less than in Mustang II days, and 1981 was the last year for the performance-flavored Cobra option. Sales couldn't match the first-year figures: 271,322 Mustangs were sold in 1980, that figure falling to 182,552 for 1981, nearly a return to Mustang II levels.

So, the new Mustang and Capri came to market in 1979 with huge fanfare and then tapered a bit. It would be unfair to label them anything other than a success, however, as the Fox platform proved to be versatile, and it accom-

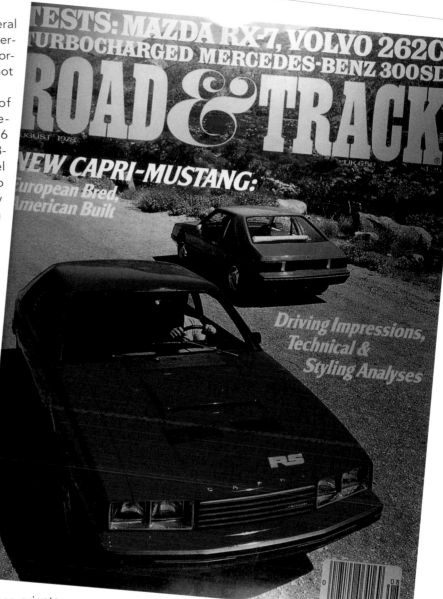

*R*oad & Track thought the new cars were important enough to warrant the cover of its August 1978 issue. The staff seemed impressed with the performance potential, rack and pinion steering, and wide array of engine choices. Mustang and Capri also seemed to be a more appealing size, from a sporty car standpoint, than the longer and heavier Camaro and Firebird. *Road & Track*

plished many of Ford's goals. But the performance-oriented driver was left wanting. Though the cars looked good and handled better than most of their competition, the turbocharged four fell far short of its billing, and the 255-cubic-inch V-8 had become a shadow of its former self.

Fortunately, good news was as close as 1982.

# *two* 5.0=Perform

# ance Reborn
## 1982-1986

Donald Petersen is a car guy. Thankfully, he was also promoted to president of Ford Motor Company in 1980. Though certain programs were already in the works by the time he took the reins, there's no doubt he was a key figure in Ford's turnaround of the mid-1980s. At the time of his appointment, we were "enjoying" yet another fuel crisis in this country, and the Mustang V-8 was only good for 120 horsepower. The Thunderbird, another Ford luxury/performance bastion, was also now based on the Fox chassis, but this turned out to be a less-than-happy mating. These "Boxbirds" were a poor followup to the hot-selling 1977–1979 models.

Petersen and company reemphasized performance with the formation of Special Vehicle Operations (see sidebar). SVO instantly gave Ford a system for developing performance-oriented parts, getting more involved in racing, and really translating some of that experience and hardware to production models. Petersen was around at Ford during Henry Ford II's

The 1982 Mustang GT was good news. The noisy and not-so-torquey turbo-four went away, at least for the moment, and the replacement was a beefier 5.0. The GT was differentiated from the prior Turbo and Cobra models by a more conservative monochromatic look, including a body-colored grille, spoiler, and no more berserk snake on the hood. You can see the ladder-type traction bars poking out from the bottom of the 1982 GT, just in front of the rear tires. The fog lights were real, not just "beauty lamps" as had been done by many manufacturers in the past. The hood scoop was nonfunctional but a bit more tasteful than the somewhat clunky unit poised atop the Capri's engine lid. The three-spoke TRX wheel was years ahead of the 1990s trend. There was some talk that the new car would be again called the Boss 302, but emulating the powerful race winner of 1969 and 1970 would have been a tall order, and Ford thought better of it. *Ford Motor Company*

"Total Performance" era of the 1960s and gave marching orders to the product development and engineering staffs to apply some of those principles to the current line-up. Fortunately, Mustang was at the top of the list to receive some help.

It would be important for the Mustang to make a good showing for 1982 as its arch rivals, the Camaro and Firebird, were going to be all new that year. The Z-28 and Trans-Am were receiving revised 305-cubic-inch V-8s to go along with their crisp new bodywork, and a special emphasis was being made to ensure better-handling, new cars.

But Ford was ready. The Mustang and Capri line-up for 1982 got a reshuffle and a good old-fashioned horsepower injection. There were few changes in terms of trim or body configurations, though the Mustang notchback got a slightly beefier B-pillar. The base four, inline six-cylinder and 255-cubic-inch V-8 engine (with automatic only) offerings remained unchanged, but things were different at the top.

Gone was the anemic 2.3-liter, carbureted turbo-four. In its place, the 5.0-liter V-8 returned. It was rated at 157 horsepower—certainly a step up from the 4.2's 120 horsepower—and was backed exclusively by a four-speed manual overdrive transmission. The previous four-speed overdrive unit did not have the torque capacity to handle the grunt of the new V-8, so this transmission—really a three-speed plus overdrive—would have to be enough for now.

How did the Ford powertrain engineers find the extra power? Simple and subtle hot-rodding methods: more air in, more air out. They reached into the marine engine parts bucket and pulled out a boat-spec camshaft, which provided the pattern for the street V-8's new cam. A new low-restriction, dual-intake air-cleaner housing meant more air in. The exhaust system was enlarged, and a low-restriction muffler allowed more air out. Credit Ford for showing some aesthetic pizzazz with the pipes as the exhaust exited the driver's-side rear fascia with a chromed twin-exhaust outlet. Best of all, it *sounded* like a V-8 again. There was also a larger two-barrel carb and some ignition recalibrations, but these straightforward modifications worked together to provide a 30-percent power increase over the 255-cubic-inch V-8 of the previous year and 17 horsepower more than the turbo-four.

For the first time in several years, Ford began paying attention to the *look* of the engine compartment. For most for the 1970s, engineering budgets were consumed by inventing and tacking on the myriad of pollution hardware necessary to meet the government's regulations. Who had time or money to worry about how the thing looked?

## FORD **MUSTANG** GT SERIES

Right: GT instrumentation.
Center: Optional Recaro bucket seat. Shown in Vaquero cloth.
Far right: Mustang GT interior with fully-reclining low-back bucket seats in Black deep-grained vinyl.
Below: Mustang GT in Silver Metallic.

The GT was a big improvement from the previous Cobra and Turbo versions. It was more conservative, and the interior was also more purposeful in its appearance. These pages from the 1982 sales brochure show the optional Recaro bucket seat, though the car is featured with the standard alloy wheel, as opposed to the optional TRX. This particular silver car must have been a very early model, probably a hand-assembled "pilot" car, as it does not have the chrome 5.0 badge on the fender. *Author collection*

But the powertrain development teams clearly wanted a real performance engine, so particular attention was paid to wire routing, material finishes, and the like. Many aluminum brackets were left in their unfinished state. The aluminum air-cleaner cover proudly proclaimed "High Output V-8," and the usual coating of Ford Blue paint was nowhere to be found. Though 1979 was technically the first application of the term "5.0-liter" for the Mustang, Five-Point-Oh faithful consider 1982 as the beginning of the 5.0 era.

It's interesting, and perhaps a bit worrisome, that this new "day of the 5.0" almost didn't happen. Many

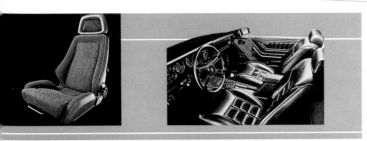

team delivered the new 5.0 in November 1981, an only slightly delayed introduction.

It certainly was the right pick: Ford's marketing strategists expected the 5.0 V-8 driveline would be ordered by 11 percent of Mustang buyers. "It was like giving candy to small children," Clarke commented wryly. "As soon as we started making them, we were shipping just about all we could. We were somewhere between 43 and 47 percent incremental volume." And to think, it almost didn't happen.

The engine/transmission combo could be ordered on plain-Jane hatchbacks and notchbacks, but the top-dog

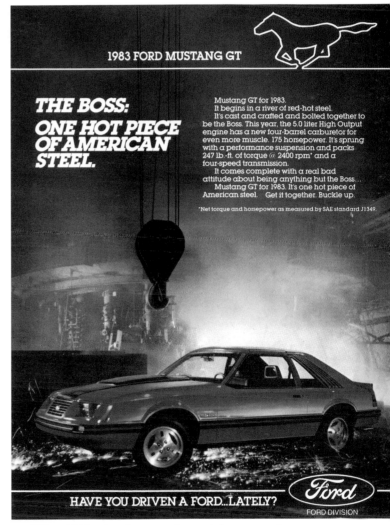

This 1983 advertisement showed the new car's revised nose treatment, additional blacked-out trim, and extra pinstriping. Whether it was an improvement over the 1982 is a matter of personal taste, but nobody had a complaint about the additional horsepower. Torque increased from 240 to 247 lb-ft and the horsepower rating went from 157 to 175, thanks to a new Holley four-barrel carb. *Author collection*

people at Ford, as with several other car makers at the time, believed the death of the big pushrod V-8 was inevitable and coming soon. Though that first trouble-wrought turbo-four of 1979 needed much work and investment to make it right, Ford believed this was the engine configuration of choice for the future and pressed ahead with its development. Carburetor problems led to the development of fuel-injected engines; however, these engines melted catalytic converters at an alarming rate and had trouble meeting emissions standards. "We were again left with the option of having only the normally aspirated four-cylinder engine for 1982," commented Jim Clarke, now chief engineer for Advanced and Preprogram Powertrain Engineering. This was in April 1981, and everyone knew that would never do. "I got a call from our general manager Dick Hagen, and I was asked if we could get another V-8 introduced into the [1982] Mustang. Well normally in April, you'd have it already. So, on one hand, we had anticipated the question, because a lot of Ford people including myself believed that a V-8 really belonged in the car, so we were mentally prepared to respond." On a limited budget and very short time, the

This factory photo of the 1985 GT shows the nicely balanced, smart but not overdone graphics, new front-end treatment, and those 10-hole alloy wheels that would serve well through the 1990 model year on V-8 powered Mustangs. Horsepower was now up to 210, and there was a revised suspension to put that power to the ground. The rear spoiler was also a new piece, smoother and rounder than the previous design. The front air intake had no grille element, and radiator air was also taken in from under the bumper area. To some, this is the best looking of the 5.0-liter Mustangs. *Ford Motor Company*

package was the new-for-1982 GT. The Cobra and Ghia options were gone, replaced by the GT moniker that had served so well on the original 1965–1966 cars. So the model line-up was alphabet soup for 1982: L, GL, GLX, and GT.

The GT package included a blockish, front spoiler with integrated fog lights, a (nonfunctional) hood scoop, and a rear-deck-lid spoiler. It was available in either black, silver, or dark metallic red. The monochromatic look was also a popular automotive theme of the day, so except for the chrome exhaust tips and 5.0 badges, no more of the shiny stuff could be found. Order the GT with the optional Recaro seating and removable glass T-roofs, and you had a special car indeed.

So how did the revitalized GT pair off against its newly dressed GM rivals? Quite well.

GM did not offer a manual transmission with the top engine—a 165-horsepower, 305-cubic-inch V-8. If you wanted a four-speed, you got a 145-horsepower V-8. Due to its drivetrain packaging and slightly lower weight, the Mustang managed to outrun either version of the Camaro. But GM's emphasis on handling paid off; while the previous Camaro was heavier and larger, the newer car was much closer to the Mustang in size. Its newly upgraded suspension and standard 15-inch performance radials gave it the edge on the twisty bits.

To the pleasure of American automotive enthusiasts, 1982 marked the rebirth of the Ford versus Chevy wars as the Mustang and Camaro (and to a lesser extent, the Firebird and Capri) began waging a performance war that has traded the advantage many times and continues to this day.

Significant changes were made to the Ford line-up in 1983. At the head of the list was an all-new Thunderbird. It was a complete design departure, even though it was once again pulled from the Fox platform. Gone was the boxy look. In its place was a rounded, sculpted shape that proved a hit with buyers and with drivers on the high-banked NASCAR tracks.

The Mustang roster also benefited from a substantial shakeup. A subtle restyling brought a new frontal aspect and a slightly revised taillight treatment. The new nose was smoother and a bit pointier with fog lights (on the GT models) deep-set into a less angular front spoiler. The GT also included a wide black paint stripe, which carried the shape of the grille across the hood to the base of the windshield. The hood scoop design was also changed but unfortunately remained nonfunctional. That's okay, though, because there were functional changes under the hood.

When Ford wanted to increase the horsepower quotient of the 289 V-8 in the original Mustangs, it bolted on a four-barrel carburetor. Again in keeping with the re-emerging "Total Performance" theme, they

It's hard to note the differences between a 1985 and a 1986 Mustang from the front, but the back is the giveaway; 1986 marked the first appearance of the Center High-Mounted Stoplight. The dual exhaust outlets remain a popular Mustang V-8 styling/performance cue since their introduction in 1985. *Ford Motor Company*

Capri swan song: 1985 was the final year for the badge-engineered Mustang. Lincoln-Mercury tried to make it distinctive by using a bubble-type rear window and different valance panels on the C-pillar while retaining the square grille and square-jawed spoiler from the earlier models. But it wasn't enough, and the Capri nameplate vanished . . . only to reappear later on an odd-looking, Mazda-based convertible that didn't last as long as the Fox-based Capris. *Ford Motor Company*

went to the same well for 1983. An emissions-engineered Holley 600-cfm carb replaced the 1982's two-barrel, atop an alloy intake manifold. The air-cleaner housing had larger intake openings, which now wore a "5.0 Liter 4V HO" label.

Inside, the engine received a roller timing chain and an even more aggressively curved, marine-derived camshaft than did the 1982. Cumulatively the changes added up to a rating of 175 horsepower. Now there was little question who would win a Mustang-Camaro runoff.

There were other changes to the powertrain roster. The age-old inline six faded away in favor of Ford's new 3.8-liter "Essex" model V-6, but the 2.3-liter four remained the base offering. The "lo-po" 255-cubic-inch V-8 was dropped for good. But in spite of the revised

and ever-more-powerful 5.0, Ford elected to put a turbo model back into the line-up.

The top model offering in the new-for-1983 Thunderbird was the Turbo Coupe. At the time, Ford was committed to the turbo-four as the performance way of the future and reengineered the Lima-based 2.3 that had proved to be a marginal engine in the 1979–1980 Mustang. Out went the carburetor, and in went a proper direct-port fuel-injection system. Though horsepower was up slightly, from 140 to 145, the new engine was smoother, and the Bosch computer-controlled injection system seemed to cure the prior unit's driveability problems.

Ford elected to also put the engine into the Mustang line-up for mid-1983 in the form of the GT Turbo. About

# Smokey Gets a Mustang

In official terms, they call them "Special Service Mustangs." In plain terms, they are intended as a tool to help law enforcement run down the lawless, haul them in, and lock them up. Or at least, write them up. And more often than not, they are used to help a stranded motorist or, occasionally, save a life.

The California Highway Patrol (CHP) had had enough. Enough of the gutless 318-powered 1980 and 1981 Dodge sedans that could not get out of their own way. While "banzai runners," as they were called at the time, prowled Mullholland Drive and deserted desert highways in hot turbo Porsches and street-converted racing machines, the CHP had to try to run them down with cars that practically needed to be going downhill to break 100 miles per hour. So the CHP and Ford got together with a plan to make use of Dearborn's hottest hardware, the new Mustang GT. These earliest cars were actually called "Severe Service Mustangs."

Getting the Mustang to meet the CHP's performance and durability requirements was not a problem. This could be accomplished with a fair minimum of requirements. The issue was a cultural one. How would the officers adapt to a car with a stick shift, the only transmission offered at the time. Instead of being able to lock a baddie in the back seat of a sedan behind a cage in a compartment with no door or window handles, what would an officer do when faced with this situation driving a two-door, notchback Mustang?

As it turned out, the CHP's experiment, conducted with 400 1982 Mustang 5.0-liter notchbacks, became a long-term relationship between Ford and numerous law enforcement agencies around the country. California's experience was so positive that the Mustang quickly became the desired property of many highway patrol officers. Naturally, they didn't have the roominess of the big police sedans, but their top speed and pursuit capability was unmatched.

Those early cars were amazingly stock. Changes included a radio interference-suppression kit, halogen headlamps, heavy-duty cooling and alternator upgrades, and, of course, the obligatory calibrated 160-mile-per-hour speedometer. As a bonus, they were also cheaper than their 1982 Impala sedan counterparts by about $1,000 ($6,868 versus $7,919 for the Chevy). Many other performance and durability improvements were added along the way: special "blue Silicone" hoses, reinforced seat frames, oil coolers, and larger wheels and tires; there were more than 100 service-unique pieces by the time the 1987 models hit the highways. The Special Service Mustangs always had the current spec V-8 performance offering, and automatic transmissions also became available. It was interesting to see some of the later cars with their 15-inch alloy wheels painted black. Some departments did not want their constituency to think they were spending money on fancy mags for their patrol cars even though the alloys were standard equipment on a 5.0 notchback.

Ford continued to offer Special Service Mustangs through the end of the Fox-bodied cars in 1993. For whatever reason, the company elected not to develop a Special Service Mustang off the 1994-and-newer platform, but perhaps they should have. In speaking with one particular CHP station, it seems the officers don't want to let them go. In fact, most CHP cars are sold off at about the 80,000-mile mark. But the last remaining batch of 1993 CHP 5.0 Mustangs have been extended to a 105,000-mile service life. Two reasons: budgetary constraints and the fact that the 5.0 Mustang is still the fastest thing with lights and a siren. Which one do you believe?

*This is certainly not a sight anyone enjoys seeing in their rearview mirror: a Mustang patrol car, red lights ablaze. What turned out to be an experiment with the California Highway Patrol resulted in 11 years worth of "special service" Mustang production. As of this writing, the last of the 1993s are still in use. To our knowledge all the police cars were notchbacks. It is possible that one or perhaps two convertibles were used in coastal areas as community-relations tools. The Mustang's compact interior still leaves enough room for the spotlights, computer, radios, clipboards, reading light, and the obligatory Winchester Defender shotgun. Matt Stone*

Notice the GT 350 striping and the running-horse emblem on this 20th Anniversary Edition Mustang. The GT 350 striping and the running-horse emblem were intended to recall great days of Mustangs past. The 20th anniversary cars did not have any rear-deck spoiler or luggage rack, contributing to a very clean look. All were equipped with the TRX wheel and tire package. All of the cars were the same white-over-red color combination. This 1984 model was their last appearance. *Scott Mead*

500 1983 GT Turbos were built. It was a pleasant enough car and delivered fuel mileage about 5 miles per gallon better than a comparable V-8 powered car, but it was still a bit rough and noisy when compared to the V-8. Being 30 horsepower down on the 5.0, and with much less torque especially at low revs, it's no wonder most buyers chose the V-8, especially considering that the Turbo cost *$250 more* than the 5.0 GT. Later installation of an intercooler helped, and the car was quite reliable.

Backing either engine was a much-needed, five-speed Borg-Warner T-5 transmission. Ford wanted the new tranny for the 1982 5.0 package, but it simply wasn't available in time, so the four-speed SROD (Single Rail Overdrive) transmission had to do for that first year. The new five-speed gave four closely spaced ratios, with fourth being a direct 1.00:1 ratio, and fifth as a genuine

overdrive. The T-5 was engineered for the V-8's power, shifted crisply and smoothly, and paired with the V-8 to create an outstanding combination. It was only a few years prior that the combination of a V-8 and a five-speed was only found in an expensive Italian exotic car. Now it could be found at your local Ford dealer. The Capri got the V-8 driveline (though the turbo was only available on the Mustang) and a bubble-shaped rear deck that was mostly glass.

Also of note was the reintroduction of the Mustang convertible in 1983. Though outside "choppers" had been converting Mustang notchbacks to ragtops since 1979, few were particularly well engineered or attractive. Ford went to one of the best in the business when it came to sunroofs and convertibles, American Sunroof Corporation (ASC).

ASC designed a power-top package that looked right and worked reasonably well. Initially ASC did the convertible conversion work at their Michigan facilities, though the job went back to Ford's Dearborn assembly plant in 1984. Part of the conversion included bracing and reinforcement of the frame to counteract the loss of torsional stiffness from cutting the top off. In unit body-chassis cars, the roof structure adds considerable strength to the entire structure. Without the additional struts and braces, the cowl-shake would have made the car virtually undriveable. In truth, the convertible version was just marginal as it was, and both racing and the aftermarket would later teach us that the Fox chassis could stand a lot of improvement in terms of structural stiffness and torsional rigidity.

The convertible could be ordered in LX V-6, LX V-8, or GT V-8 form. In response to the handling challenge presented by the new-for-1982 Camaro, the Mustang got wider TRX tires for improved grip. All in all, the Mustang became a much-improved American performance car in this one model year with an uprated V-8, five-speed gearboxes, a fuel-injected turbocharged engine option, and a new convertible. Advertisements proclaimed "Ford's back" and "The Boss is Back." It seemed true enough.

With the introduction of the 1984 cars, the Mustang was essentially a carryover model. The biggest news was the introduction of the Mustang SVO (see sidebar), but a few other interesting things occurred along the way. As good as the new five-speed transmission was, a portion of the market prefers, or demands, an automatic transmission. Ford responded to this demand by introducing an automatic GT. The automatic-spec engine was a bit different in that it carried a throttle-body fuel-injection system instead of the Holley four-barrel carb. It was backed by Ford's four-speed automatic overdrive (4AOD) transmission. All 1984 Fords received the company's new EEC-IV computerized electronic engine-management system. EEC-IV went a long way toward allowing the engines to offer ever-increasing performance while meeting emissions and fuel-economy requirements. It should be noted that EEC-IV was also used, in practically stock form, on many Ford race cars in the late 1980s.

Horsepower for the automatic-equipped V-8 Mustangs was down a bit from 175 to 165, but it mattered little. The automatic buyer was probably not interested in maximum acceleration anyway, and it still made those great V-8 noises.

In honor of the Mustang's 20th birthday, a special edition model was introduced (commemorative models were de riguer in the 1980s). It was available in either convertible or notchback form so as not to steal any thunder from the hatchback-only SVO. In typical Henry Ford fashion, customers could have any color they wanted, in this case, as long as it was white with red interior and trim.

The Twentieth Anniversary or Commemorative Edition Mustang was fitted with either the turbo-four, automatic-equipped V-8 or the five-speed, 5.0 HO. One curious addition, besides the expected commemorative badging, was the red "GT 350" striping along the rocker panels just like those found on the first Shelby Mustangs. The model wasn't built by Shelby; it wasn't officially called a GT 350; and it certainly didn't perform like one. So what gives? Perhaps a bit of overmarketeering or a minor slip in tastefulness by the stylists.

For 1985, Ford was clearly pursuing two different tacks with the Mustang. The upmarket offering, with an emphasis on handling and technical specification, was the SVO. Yet the standard 5.0 got its share of attention with another face-lift, more engine upgrades, and more horsepower.

Changes for 1985 were probably the most sweeping the car had received since its introduction in 1979. The Mustang got yet another new nose with a clean radiator opening instead of the previous egg-crate grilles. The nonfunctioning, somewhat superfluous, bolt-on hood scoop was eliminated, and the perimeter rub-strip now included "GT" identification just aft of the door openings. A less angular rear spoiler adorned the deck lid. The interior enjoyed some rub-off from the SVO in the form of a handsome three-spoke steering wheel and a dash that attempted to achieve an aircraft look with modular housings surrounding the gauges. It is lauded by some as the best-looking Mustang of the post-1979 era.

Engine options were once again shuffled. The turbo-four option, even in its improved form, never proved popular. With the turbocharged SVO now in the line-up, there was no need for a Turbo GT version, so it bowed out quietly at the end of the 1984 season. Now clearly focused on the V-8, it was time for another round of engine improvements and more ponies for the pony.

The valvetrain on the 1985-spec 5.0 was upgraded to a roller cam and tappets, which increased reliability, reduced friction, and was easier running at high rpm. The engine benefited from more aggressive cam timing, as Ford was learning how to get the most out of the new EEC engine controls. But perhaps the biggest gains came in the exhaust department. While the previous system flowed reasonably well, it was still comprised of cast-iron manifolds, a single catalytic converter, muffler, and exhaust pipe. Ford's engine development team threw away the pipes and started over from the engine back.

Steel tube headers replaced the heavy and restrictive iron manifolds, and a full dual exhaust system was implemented. This included two catalytic converters, two mufflers, and polished stainless pipes exiting out the back. The result was better breathing, better looks, and an even better sound.

# 1984-1986 Mustang SVO:

## The Little Engine That (Almost) Could

Ford didn't really fool anyone when it announced the formation of its Special Vehicle Operations function in 1981. Apply whatever moniker you wish, the birth of SVO was the racing department's coming out party. SVO's main thrusts were to develop a line of performance and racing parts, then field or back racing teams that could take those goodies to the track and win. A "factory aftermarket" catalog of parts and accessories would stem from it. American manufacturers' racing programs had been running tepid, and enough was enough. Ford CEO Donald Petersen brought Michael Kranefuss home from Germany where he had prior experience with Ford of Europe racing programs, gathered up 30 or so of Ford's most enthusiastic car people, and told them to *go for it*. Championships in IMSA/SportsCar, SCCA, NHRA, and NASCAR are testimony to their success.

What better way to trumpet this new group's arrival than to let them build their own special model. According to an early internal document, SVO noticed "broadened consumer awareness of 'European' handling traits and performance-combined-with-economy from small-displacement engines. With this awareness has come a demand in America for performance cars in the European idiom." Buzzwords included "exceptional quality, economy, performance, and road manners." Ford's target: the BMW 318i. Their weapon: an SVO version of the Mustang.

SVO was handed a challenge in that budgetary and production limitations dictated the existing Mustang platform be used. SVO went to work and packed the car with the best hardware it could muster. To be marketed as a virtually complete, no-options car (there were a few things that could be owner-specified), the SVO was available in hatchback form only beginning with the 1984 model year. In keeping with the performance-from-small-displacement goal, SVO revised the Thunderbird Turbo Coupe's 2.3-liter four by adding an intercooler and came up with 175 horsepower. The only available transmission was a beefy Borg-Warner five-speed topped by a Hurst shifter. The suspension featured Koni gas-charged shocks, a quicker steering gear, and four-wheel disc brakes (the SVO was the first Mustang to have these). The Corvette was not the only 1984 model to make the move to the 16-inch wheel/tire combo that now seems so common; the SVO was riding on Euro-spec 225/50-16 Goodyear NCTs that same year.

The look had to be right, speaking of both performance and sophistication. Ford did a rather tasteful job in this arena, giving the car a smooth, virtually grille-less nose with a wrap-around light cluster, subtle spats in front of the rear wheels, revised "gills" aft of the rear windows, and two somewhat controversial styling/performance elements: an intake for the intercooler that was offset toward the passenger side of the hood and a unique bi-wing deck spoiler.

The passenger compartment received similar upgrading with terrific sport seats, full instrumentation, and one other interesting high-tech goodie—a console-mounted switch, allowing the driver to reprogram the engine-management system for either regular or premium fuel.

The SVO received one fairly substantial upgrading during its three-year life. In mid-1985, the engine received revised cam specs, a new intake manifold, full dual exhausts, and a different turbocharger. The Pinto-derived four-banger was now pumping out 205 horsepower. The 1986 models would be dialed back a tad to 200. Springs, bushings, and roll bars were recalibrated for better handling. The front end finally got the flush headlights it was begging for, and the last SVOs had a conventional spoiler on the rear deck.

*The Mustang SVO looked considerably different than the standard car and hinted at future Mustang styling cues. Features like flush headlight glass and 16-inch wheels would appear in 1987 and 1991, respectively. Note the air intake for the turbo-four's intercooler, which was asymmetrically placed toward the passenger side of the hood.* Matt Stone

On the road, the package worked well enough. The turbo-four doesn't offer much at low revs; boost shows up at around 2,500 rpm, and then the power comes on with a bang at about 3,000. From there, it's a quick, strong pull up to 6,000 rpm. It's not the sweetest trip; however, the engine produced noise and vibration matching its hefty power output. Some consider the SVO to be the best-handling Fox-platformed Mustang ever, the lighter engine giving it slightly better balance than its V-8 powered brethren. The SVO certainly was faster than the 3-series Bimmer but couldn't quite match the overall quality feel and tactile sophistication of its pricier Teutonic target.

Ford never intended the SVO to be a high-volume model; it was priced about $2,500 above a comparably equipped and V-8 powered GT 5.0. Still, a certain population was willing to ante the difference for the exclusivity and upgrades. Many of the SVO's features showed up later on standard Mustangs (flush headlights in 1987, 16 inch wheels/tires in 1991). Others, such as the four-wheel disc package, should have. Still, Ford was readying its 225-horsepower, 5.0-liter Mustang and a faster, more sophisticated Thunderbird Turbo Coupe for 1987. Rather than compete with itself, Ford wisely wrapped up SVO production at the end of 1986. Before it was over, Ford built 9,844 SVOs, and they have become among the more collectable Mustangs.

The 175-horse 5.0 breathed in through a dual-snorkel air filter that was shared with the LTD police cars. Note the use of factory-installed, finned, alloy valve covers, a far cry from the old stamped-steel units liberally coated with Ford Blue paint. This particular car is an automatic-equipped GT, identifiable because all automatic-equipped cars for 1983 and 1984 had throttle-body fuel injection instead of the Holley four-barrel. *Scott Mead*

This approach was nothing new. Hot rodders had been slipping in stouter cams and welding on dual exhausts for years. The 5.0 really responded. Horsepower improved 20 percent to 210 at 4,600 rpm. Equally important was the new torque rating of 265 lb-ft at only 3,400 rpm. Simply put, it made for the fastest Mustang since the Boss 351 days of more than a dozen years before.

The automatic-equipped V-8 also earned a boost to 180 horsepower. And the 1985 chassis was updated as well. When it was introduced, the Michelin TRX tire system was as good as it got. But the market never sits still, and by the mid-1980s several brands were offering high-quality, high-performance 15-inch tires.

Goodyear, in particular, had developed their "Gatorback" design—patterned after its racing Blue Streaks. Ford customers were also not always happy about having to buy only Michelin tires for a TRX-equipped car, especially when stranded in an area not exactly overrun with Michelin dealers. They had accomplished their mission

from 1979–1984, but for 1985, Ford moved on to a new and conventionally sized 15x7-inch alloy wheel. Ford specified Goodyear's latest 225/60-15 Eagle VR60 tires for the new Mustang and Capri, and they were an ideal match for the handsome new "10 hole" wheel.

Other changes in the suspension department included gas-pressurized shock absorbers front and rear and a second set of shocks mounted to the rear axle. The additional units were set at a different angle than the main shocks to control axle wind-up during hard acceleration. This arrangement is colloquially referred to as "quad shock." The Mustang was now putting out some substantial horsepower (compared to the original 140 that the chassis was designed for) and axle-hop continued to be a problem. Thank goodness there was horsepower to make it hop. In road tests the Mustang could reel off 0–60 times in the low 7-second range, and top speed was a genuine 140-plus. The new tires, wheels, and suspension treatments all increased the Mustang's cornering prowess substantially, though the best underpinnings (16-inch wheels, four-wheel disc brakes) were saved for the SVO.

One thing was clear: It could still outrun the Chevys. *Road & Track* staged a runoff with a 1985 Mustang GT (one of the first hand-assembled pilot cars) and a 190-horsepower Camaro IROC-Z. The Chevrolet was equipped with the Borg-Warner T-5 five-speed and a 16-inch wheel and tire package. The results are not surprising, considering the Mustang's lighter weight and greater horsepower and the Camaro's larger rolling stock and newer suspension setup. "This is a case of you pick 'em," said the *R & T* testers. "The Mustang won the acceleration round and had an edge in braking. But the Camaro slugged its way to the top in the other rounds (handling, braking, looks). Both champions put up a great battle and we're not sure we could pick an absolute winner. On a short course, where handling is important, the title would go to the IROC-Z. On a long course where horsepower and high speed count, the crown would probably go to the Mustang GT."

A review of 1986 finds Mustang in a transitional year. From an appearance standpoint, the cars were much the same as they were in 1985. Under the category of mandated changes was the center-high-mounted brake light, recessed into the rear-deck spoiler. Overall, however, the Mustang was visually similar to the original 1979 models. Under the hood it was a different story, one that would affect Mustang powerplants for the next 10 years.

By the mid-1980s, the carburetor was going the way of the dodo. It was increasingly difficult to make this long-standing method of fuel metering pass muster when it came to fuel economy and emissions performance. Advances in electronic engine management and the development of fuel injection led to hardware that could outperform the old four-barrel. So, as much as the Holley 600 did to juice the power output of the 5.0 as recently as 1983, it was headed for the dumpster at the end of the 1985 model year.

In its place was a new fuel-injection unit that had made its appearance on the V-8 Thunderbird and a few other Ford models the year before—not a throttle-body unit like the ones on the automatic-equipped 5.0s, but a direct-port-injection design that featured an upper and lower intake manifold, computerized fuel metering, and a mass air-sensing device. Depending upon the size of the actual fuel injectors, the pressure of the fuel pump, the size of the air intake, and other factors, the Ford fuel-injection system could be tuned for optimum amounts of power, economy, or both. Another by-product of the system was the promise of crisper throttle response and an easier time of dealing with future emissions requirements. It seemed like a good thing.

And it was. Though power output was reduced slightly from 210 to 200 horsepower due to use of a "mashed-valve" cylinder head for 1986 only, driveability was dramatically improved. While nobody likes a horsepower decrease, and we'd seen them before, there was an increase in torque from 265 lb-ft to 285. In street driving, it's the torque that really moves the car. So in some instances, the injected car actually felt more powerful than the carbureted version.

The previous 180-horse, throttle-body 5.0 was discontinued, so folks who specified the four-speed automatic transmission got the 200-horsepower engine as well. Sound-deadening was improved, new engine mounts meant less vibration, and a new and much stronger 8.8-inch rear end added value.

Although the SVO Mustang was somewhat successful, it fell short of its ultimate potential, and 1986 was its final production year. The car that enthusiasts *really wanted* had the SVO packaging—including features like the 16-inch wheels and tires, four-wheel disc brakes, flush headlamps, and leather interior—along with the 200- or 210-horsepower version of the 5.0 V-8. Sales for 1986 reached 224,410 cars, a substantial increase of nearly 75,000 units compared to 1985.

That mythical SVO V-8 never happened. But Ford's plan for the 1987 Mustang gave buyers a little bit of each and something more. Can you count to 225?

Ford's interior-design stylists intended the 1993–1994 dash to resemble aircraft instrumentation. The nacelles around the instruments look as if each gauge was a separate, modular piece. In truth, it was all a single piece of plastic; even the Allen-head screws were fake. But the look was good enough. The gold badge on the dash signifies this as a 20th Anniversary Mustang. Note the original warranty service booklet. *Scott Mead*

# *three* Fox Heyday

# 1987-1993

The 1987 Mustang could be called the Mustang that almost wasn't. As early as 1982, it seemed clear to Ford that while the Fox platform was versatile, simple to construct, and cost effective, front-wheel drive would be the wave of the future. Front-wheel drive is more efficient from a driveline packaging standpoint and made it even easier to build different cars off the same platform. Sure, shoehorning a big V-8 into a front-wheel-drive chassis might be tough, but someday rear-wheel drive would be old-fashioned anyway, right? Or so Ford and most every other American manufacturer thought at the time.

Just as those first reborn 5.0-liter HO GT Mustangs were hitting the market, Ford began work on a platform known internally as SN8. The SN8 code was the designation for a front-wheel-drive platform larger than that of the world car Escort, which came out just the year before. The idea was for SN8 to take on those Celicas, Preludes, and other sporty coupes where they live. Many of the well-known automotive enthusiast magazines also predicted rear-wheel-drive honkers were about to be history, so Ford's move seemed to make sense.

They didn't count on two things: a genuine resurgence of the performance market, particularly for V-8 engines, and the resources available to them from their Japanese stepchild, Mazda. Fuel injection and electronic engine-management systems allowed V-8s to increase fuel mileage, maintain emissions

End of the line: The last of the Fox-bodied Mustang GTs were produced for 1993. It looked much as it did when last revised in 1987, though by this time the monochromatic appearance was in fashion. There were no more pinstripes, and the recessed protective molding had also given up its colored stripes. Two-tone paint schemes had been axed, and the GT shared the five-spoke alloy wheels with the LX model. *Ford Motor Company publicity photo*

The last of the Fox-bodied Mustangs were about horsepower and performance-value for the money. The younger performance crowd couldn't tell you much about a flathead or a 302, but they do know their Five Point Oh. *Matt Stone*

requirements, *and* deliver better performance, all at the same time. Buyers responded to more powerful Mustangs (and Capris, Camaros, and Firebirds), as all the pony cars posted increasing sales numbers.

In addition, Ford partnered with Mazda to develop front-wheel-drive platforms that would serve both automakers. Ford owned approximately 25 percent of Mazda at the time.

A front-wheel-drive, four-cylinder-powered, Japanese-flavored Mustang? Excuse me? Didn't Ford learn its lesson with the Mustang II episode? Apparently not. Strange as it may seem, plans were afoot to replace the Fox-bodied Mustang with a Ford-Mazda joint-venture car for the 1988 or 1989 model year. How that *didn't* happen is a worthy subject for a book. Thankfully, it was finally decided that Ford would continue the front-wheel-drive program with Mazda, but the resulting product would be sold alongside the rear-wheel-drive Mustang and not in place of it (see sidebar titled "Ford Probe: Nearly The Next Mustang").

The final decision came down in 1985, a time when the Mustang needed updating beyond the minor but continuous improvements the car had received from 1982–1986.

The entire line-up was shuffled. Though fastback, notchback, and convertible body styles would remain, the packaging was reconciled into models that made more sense and emphasized the V-8 drivelines. First, the SVO bowed out. This project wasn't entirely unsuccessful, but few folks were willing to pay more for a four-cylinder car that wasn't as powerful as the Mustang GT, no matter how much more sophisticated the balance of the package was. The Pinto-based turbo-four, even the later 200- and 205-horsepower versions, never possessed the smoothness and low-end torque to match the SVO's trim levels and balance.

Additionally, the Capri was cut. Sales had been floundering, and there was not enough content to differentiate it from its Mustang counterparts. It no longer had much in common with the smaller, lighter cars built in Europe; that's what most people thought of when they thought of Capri. Have you ever wondered what might have happened if Ford had taken the SVO package, further improved the European-inspired drivetrain, kept the appearance distinct from the Mustang, kept the emphasis on sharp-edged handling, perhaps removed some content and lowered the price . . . and called the package the 1987 Mercury Capri SVO? It might have worked. But by then, Mercury dealers already had the Merkur XR4Ti to sell.

So Capri and the SVO Mustang were gone. With that, Ford elected to split the V-8-powered Mustang line-up in two: the GT, which was established to be the top model, and the 5.0 LX, a sort of Plymouth Road Runner version packing the V-8 driveline with a minimum of dress-up items and less feature content than the GT. The 1986 models were the last to offer the 3.8-liter V-6 engine (until much later, that is). So

The 1987–1993 GT's "cheese grater" taillight treatment is a "love it or hate it" feature among Mustang enthusiasts. Some GT owners have even gone so far as to swap in LX or even tri-colored SVO taillights to replace these units. This car is a 1992 model; note the license plate. *Matt Stone*

for 1987 it was either four-cylinders or eight. The mid-level models had not been selling well anyway. Many of the lighter, newer-designed Japanese cars would handily out perform them. But the four-banger hung around to increase CAFE and, in the words of one journalist, "keep the Mustang popular with rental fleets and secretaries." At least it finally got fuel injection to replace the nearly archaic carburetor.

The GT received a new nose treatment with flush headlights and a "bottom breather" intake design. The lower front fascia also held new, round fog lights. The lower cladding and rocker panel areas were sculpted to create what appeared to be little air intakes; the only problem was, from a functional standpoint, they didn't take the air anywhere. The design was actually supposed to funnel air into both

# Ford Probe: Nearly the Next Mustang

Ford had owned a 25-percent stake in Mazda since 1979, curiously the same year that the Fox-bodied Mustang came to market. The Japanese were good at developing fuel-efficient, four-cylinder automobiles and also had the jump on implementing the flourishing move to front-wheel drive. The two companies were anxious to make use of their partnership, so a joint-venture development program to develop a front-wheel-drive sporty coupe began in 1982. Running prototypes were on the road by late 1985. Dubbed SN8, the project was to yield the 626 sports coupe for Mazda—and the new 1988 or 1989 Mustang for Ford.

It seems crazy from today's standpoint, in light of 305-horsepower Cobras, that Ford would even consider turning the Mustang into a front-wheel-drive, four-cylinder car built in connection with a Japanese company. But according to Janine Bay, chief program engineer for Mustang, "That's what people were doing at the time. That's the way we, and everyone else in the business, thought the market was heading." GM was making noise that the Camaro/Firebird was headed toward a V-6, front-wheel-drive design. "There was a reluctance to want to add nameplates as well," said Bay. "There was a strong desire to want to 'play in that playground' and some people said 'well maybe Mustang is a name we could put on it.'" Ford also knew the Fox platform couldn't last forever. But it didn't count on performance cars returning to popularity, nor did the corporate planners expect fuel prices to remain relatively cheap. Above all, Ford underestimated the power of both press and pen.

We don't know who started it, but several automotive journalists got a hold of the notion, as well as spy photos of the "Maztang" prototypes, and told everyone that the V-8 Mustang's day was done. *AutoWeek*, for example, broke a cover story in April 1987 showing amazingly accurate photos of the car, predicting the Fox-bodied Mustang would exit "around 1990, a year or so after the Mazstang debuts."

There were at least four groups of supporters who were outraged at the notion: Mustang enthusiasts, several Ford dealers, much of the automotive media, and a considerable faction within Ford itself. *Mustang Monthly* mounted a letter-writing campaign to "Save The Mustang." *MM*'s editor Donald Farr wrote, "The descendants of the '79 Mustang, namely the GTs, pulled the Mustang name out of the ditch that was dug by the Mustang II. And now, after the Mustang has clawed its way to the top of the pony car heap once again, Ford plans to turn it into a front-wheel-drive copy of a Japanese car. Un-American, I say." Dealers also complained, and some of the more impassioned owners threatened never to buy another Ford product. Letters poured in. It was the best revolt since the Boston Tea Party. And to Ford's credit, it listened.

On August 27, 1987, just four months after the *AutoWeek* article appeared, Ford announced that "Probe" had been the name selected for a sporty new front-wheel-drive coupe to be sold beginning in mid-1988 as a 1989 model. In a November 1987 interview with *WARD'S*, Ford divisional general manager Robert Rewey said, "Probe is more in line with Japanese-type cars like [Toyota's] Celica. It won't cannibalize our other lines." But it almost did.

This is also the reason the Mustang's 1987 remodel stayed on the market so long (seven model years). Ford anticipated that Probe would replace it, so there was no need to have another product development program in process. Once it was decided that Probe would be sold along-side the Mustang, the study team lead by John Coletti was formed that would begin work on the Fox's replacement for 1994.

Mustang survived, but it was too close a call for comfort.

*The Mustang that almost was. Thankfully, smarter heads at Ford listened to outcries from its buyers, the aftermarket manufacturers, the Mustang press, Ford dealers, and even Ford employees who knew that a front-wheel-drive, four-cylinder Mustang just wouldn't be right. Ford Motor Company publicity photo*

The preeminent "bang for buck" value of the late 1980s and early 1990s, the LX 5.0 Sport. At about 200 pounds lighter than the GT due to less plastic cladding, a smaller rear wing, no fog lights, etc., performance was actually a bit better than the top-of-the line GT model. A revised 1987–1993 front end incorporated a slightly smaller air intake than the 1985–1986 cars and flush headlamps. Though they resembled the 1985 1/2–1986 SVO units, they were actually completely different components. This 1991 model was the first to feature the new 16-inch wheel. A new rear window and C-pillar eliminated the plastic insert "gill." Though the gill could be changed to give an updated styling treatment, this design was smoother, quieter, and less rust-prone than the older look. Though barely visible, this car features the factory flip-up glass sunroof. *Matt Stone*

the front and rear brakes, but experts have said it really just passed beneath the plastic, doing nothing for brake cooling in the process. Some would say the scoops were also a less than stylistic triumph.

Another exterior restyling change is generally considered for the better. The rear side windows, which previously consisted of a slightly recessed, non-functional side window and a plastic gill/grille adorning the C-pillar, were replaced by a larger, flush-mounted piece of glass. This reduced wind noise and smoothed the side appearance. The "MUSTANG" logotype was screened onto the glass as a nice styling touch. The rain gutters and front door window frames were also redesigned for a smoother look. Many owners

of 1979–1986 Mustangs have retrofitted the flush glass to their older cars.

Also the topic of some debate was the new look for the rear end of the GT. The lower rear fascia was rather blockish and did away with the polished, dual exhaust pipes that were added two years previously. Oh, there were still dual exhausts, but they now exited underneath the panel. The taillights got a hot rod-inspired louvered treatment, as if the taillight lens was made of metal, then taken to a body shop and "punched" full of louvers. Though certainly aggressive, some liked them, and some didn't. The GT also received a new 20-spoke alloy wheel design, though it retained the 15x7-inch size of the previous mag. Tire sizes were unchanged.

Ford's Mustang body style roster for 1987 can be seen in this sales brochure shot. The notchback (top) was available only in LX form (never offered as a GT), while the convertible and fastback coupe could be ordered either way. Note the differences in the wheels, the GT featuring the new-for-1987 spoke design, while the LX retained the previous 10-hole alloy. *Author collection*

The 1987–1993 GT featured scoops in the lower body cladding, but racers say they provided no brake-cooling effect whatsoever and served only as a stylistic touch. This photo comes from the 1987 sales brochure. Note the slated screen over the rear-deck window, an item that was not offered on production models. *Author collection*

This 1987 sales brochure photo shows details of the new dash. While some still favor the older, flat style, there's no getting around the ergonomic improvements of the new design. The switchgear was easier to reach and operate, and the twist controls for the Heating, Ventilation, and Air Conditioning system (HVAC) were easier to adjust while driving. The gauges were now backlit and much easier to read at night. Note that the cruise-control switches are on the steering wheel instead of being on the difficult-to-use, "broken chicken wing" stalk found on the GM cars. *Author collection*

The new model was the LX 5.0, and Ford probably didn't count on it becoming quite so popular with the performance set as it did. The LX got the same driveline as the GT but sans the spoilers and cladding. That meant no driving lights, a slightly more conventional grille, and the use of the older style alloy wheel. The effect was a slightly more conservative look. It also meant the shiny exhaust pipes stayed. More significant to the performance buyer, the LX was about 200 pounds *lighter* than the top-line GT. Everyone knows that less weight means more performance. Like the Plymouth Road Runner of nearly two decades before, the less-costly 5.0 LX would outperform the more-expensive GT model. The 5.0 LX could be had in hatchback, notchback, and convertible form, while the GT was reserved for the hatchback and ragtop models only.

Regardless of your opinion about LX versus GT styling, most everyone agreed Mustang's new-for-1987 interior was a big improvement. The dash layout was completely revised with the six main instruments set into a nacelle directly in front of the driver. The headlights, fog lights (GT models), emergency flasher, and rear-window defogger were now controlled via paddle switches, not unlike those first seen on the Isuzu Impulse. The gauges were now backlit and considerably easier to read than the previous instruments. Controls for the Heating, Ventilation, and Air Conditioning system (HVAC) were also revised to a new easy-to-use twist dial setup.

The GT benefited from excellent multi-adjustable seats, though the LX had to make due with the "rental car" benches, at least for this year. Seat fabrics and door panel treatments also got a freshening. Though a few diehards still liked the look of the older, flatter dash, few would argue that the new one was a functional improvement. But the big news, or big noise, when it comes to musclecars is always under the hood. Again the Mustang took a big leap ahead. The 1987 round of revisions centered around an updated 5.0-liter V-8, rated at 225 horsepower at 4,000 rpm, with a robust 300 lb-ft of torque at 3,000 revs.

How did Ford come up with the extra ponies? A little parts bin juggling. They took the new-for-1986 speed-density fuel-injection system and mated it to a set of pre-1986 heads offering better airflow. The combo was good for another 25 horses. All the more recent improvements, such as the roller tappets, roller rocker arms, and EEC-IV engine-management system remained in place.

There were a myriad of other changes that made the Mustang a much-improved car. Larger 10.9-inch front discs from the Lincoln Continental luxury sedan

Airbags made their appearance on the 1991 models, but Ford managed to keep the cruise-control buttons on the wheel. The wheel was even wrapped in leather. Additional gauges in place of the center air vents and the leather shift knob are aftermarket pieces. *Author collection*

replaced the previous 10.1-inch units, and the front suspension calibrations were changed for improved handling. The live axle in back carried over the SVO's four-shock arrangement, doing its best to keep the rear end in place during bumpy cornering maneuvers. A four-speed automatic transmission option was offered, and it was finally matched to the 225-horsepower engine.

The new 5.0 really delivered the mail; 0–60 times for GTs ranged in the low-to-mid-6.0-second range, with quarter-mile times in the low 15s. The LX, which was lighter, was even a tick quicker. A good-running, well-driven LX 5.0 on a cool day could easily bust into the 14s.

A few of the SVO's pieces could have, and should have, found their way into the 1987 Mustangs, namely its 16-inch wheels and four-wheel disc brakes. The Camaro had both, including an aggressive 245/50ZR16 tire package. The Chevrolet's chassis was really no better than the Ford's, but a bit lower center of gravity and the beefier rolling stock always let it turn in higher skid-pad numbers than the Mustang. Apparently Ford stopped short for budgetary reasons . . . strange when the parts were already developed and had appeared on the SVO for three years.

*Road & Track* seems to enjoy holding Mustang versus Camaro showdowns and did so in 1987 to once again compare the revised Mustang with its long-time nemesis. The test Camaro was a 220-horse-power V-8, automatic-equipped car, and the Mustang was a new GT five-speed. They seemed more than a match: "Acceleration results were as predictable as a sunrise. If, instead of comparing the Ford and Chevy, we had tested either two Mustangs or two Camaros, we would have gotten results no closer. Up to 90 miles per hour, the Mustang pulls out only the slightest advantage because of its lower weight. This disappears by 100 miles per hour as the Camaro gains an aerodynamic advantage of the tiniest proportions. Mustang and Camaro drivers will be able to spend entire days making runs at a drag strip without determining a clear winner, which should make for lots of happy drag racers and spectators."

The skid pad gave the nod to the Chevrolet, however, with steady cornering rates of 0.85 g (there's those tires again!) as compared to the Mustang's 0.80 g. While the *R & T* testers liked the feel of the Mustang's more precise steering, the Camaro IROC-Z still took the points in the handling contest. The same goes for braking, where the Chevrolet's four-wheel discs provided more consistent stops than the Mustang's disc/drum combo. The Mustang did pick up points in terms of packaging with more headroom, better visibility, better rear leg room, and more storage spaces . . . advantages it still holds over the Camaro today.

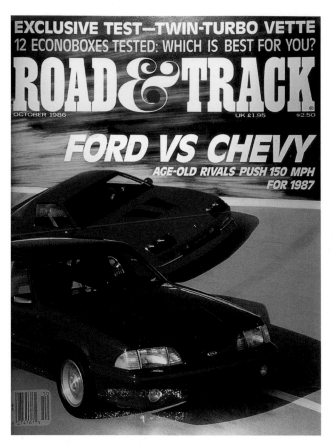

Mustang and Camaro were most evenly matched from 1987 through 1992. Many magazines staged an annual runoff between the two. It is interesting to note how close the acceleration and top-speed performances are. In one magazine the Mustang would be faster. In another magazine, on another day and at another track with different drivers, the Camaro would win. This was as good as the "Ford versus Chevy" battle ever got. *Road & Track*

The Camaro got the win by the slimmest of margins, but the test proved the Mustang and Camaro were perhaps better matched than ever before. Top speed? Again another virtual tie with the Chevy just nipping the Ford by *0.9 miles per hour* . . . as in 148.1 versus 149.2. Close enough.

But all of the above number crunching should not be allowed to pass without the review of one more set of numbers. The Mustang carried an as-tested price of $12,548, as compared to the Camaro's wallet-flattening $18,179 estimated sticker. So, even though performance was within a point here and a tick there, the Camaro cost nearly *50 percent more*. Need any further evidence as to why the 1987–1993 Mustang has been called the best bang-for-buck car of recent times?

Given the substantial remodeling for 1987, you'd expect 1988 to be a carryover year, and it was. Still,

the market reacted well to the new car, and 1988 sales figures eclipsed 1987s by just over 50,000 units (159,145 versus 211,225).

Although 1989 was much the same, it could—and perhaps should—have been more. The LX 5.0 became more of a stand-alone model, now officially called the LX 5.0 Sport, as its sales were actually outstripping that of the GT, though that may be partially due to law enforcement sales. The LX also got the GT's multi-adjustable front seats for 1989, a welcome improvement from the pool-table-flat buckets of the previous base model.

Mechanical changes included minor revisions to the suspension, including gas-pressurized struts and mildly revised spring rates in the rear. The 5.0-liter V-8 also received an engineering revision to the intake system. The 1987 and 49-state 1988 Mustang 5.0's fuel-injection system used an air measurement system called "speed-density." The design was changed for 1989 (California cars actually got them in 1988) to a new system called "mass air." The mass air system reads air intake more accurately than the speed density design. Though horsepower was unchanged at 225, the mass air system is much easier to modify—an important step in terms of aftermarket and performance upgrading. The mass air system can be swapped out for a larger one, a plan that adheres to the dictum that the key to more power is "more air and fuel in, more air out."

It appeared the "Probe scare" was over, at least for the time being, so Ford elected to make some capital improvements to the Mustang's assembly plant in Dearborn. The upgrades to the line ran more than $200 million, hopefully underscoring that the Mustang would be around for a while.

The question most frequently asked in 1989 was: Had it really been a quarter of a century since that first 1964-1/2 model hit the streets? Indeed it had, and Ford had a golden opportunity for a 25th Anniversary model. Just as they did when they needed a 1979 Indy Pace Car Mustang, Ford went to Jack Roush and company, toying with the idea of delivering an oh-so special Mustang for the silver anniversary.

The Roush 25th Anniversary prototype was a 1988 GT fastback that Roush worked over in terms of both appearance and performance. There were no changes to the interior, but the exterior was a tasteful monochromatic red with lower rocker panel ground-effects treatment. The front fascia was also an aftermarket piece, again with a cleaner look, and a grille covering the lower air intake. Instead of fog lights, the spoiler had dual air intakes to draw air into the twin intercoolers.

The 1992 LX 5.0 Sport convertible was also the body style favored for several limited-edition models at the end of the Fox run, including all white, monochromatic red, and monochromatic yellow combinations. Note the luggage rack and CHMSL. *Matt Stone*

Intercoolers? Intercoolers (plural) usually mean turbochargers (plural). Correct. In this instance the Roush special featured a twin-turbo, fuel-injection 351-cubic-inch Windsor V-8. The intake system was especially unique, as it somewhat resembled a Boeing 737 jet when viewed from above. It used twin Garrett turbos and featured waste gates to bleed off excessive boost. The installation looked all but production ready; the Roush-developed 5.8-liter engine package was said to be good for *well over* 400 horsepower in prototype form. Even when detuned for production and reliability purposes, power output could have easily been an emissions-legal 375 to 380 horsepower. The Roush special also wore serious-looking 17-inch, multi-spoked alloy wheels with wider-than-stock rubber. It was an impressive-looking, and supposedly impressive-performing, piece, one that would have ended the Mustang versus Camaro (and Corvette, for that matter) controversy once, if not for all.

So why didn't they build it? Several reasons—all unofficial, because from an official standpoint, no such car ever existed, at least as a *factory authorized* 25th Anniversary model. First, of course, was cost. The engine would have had to have been emissions-certified, an expensive process. Secondly, there was another type of cost, as in "how much will a Mustang buyer pay." Totally unofficial guesstimates would

Though the convertible and hatchback coupe body styles are more popular and perhaps a bit more stylish, there's a lot to be said for the notchback coupe. For one, it's a stiffer body shell, so inherent handling capability is higher. It's also a few pounds lighter than the other body configurations, and some people—like the California Highway Patrol, who first chose them for high-speed highway duty in 1982—enjoy a regular trunk. Used patrol cars have become popular bargains for those looking to get into a 5.0 Mustang for minimum dollars. Many ex-service Mustangs ended up as weekend club racers and quarter-mile "bracket" cars. *Matt Stone*

have priced the car well into the $30,000 range, which seemed like a lot for a Mustang back in 1989. A third reason might have been CAFE. Even though such a car would have surely been a limited-edition model, all figure into a manufacturer's fuel-efficiency rating. Need I say twin-turbo V-8s are not known for fuel economy? If the Special Vehicle Team was around at that time (its first car would not come until 1993), would the 25th Anniversary twin-turbo actually have been built? It's all speculation at this point.

There was also some debate within Ford as to which year was really the Mustang's 25th anniversary anyway. The original came out in April 1964, but the first full year of sales was 1965. So depending upon the desired marketing spin, the 25th anniversary year could be 1989 or

The 25th Anniversary Mustang that could have been. Jack Roush built this prototype in 1988, and it remains in his collection today. The subtle body modifications did away with the lower side air scoops as seen on the 1987–1993 GT. This car certainly resembles the first SVT Cobra that would come along five years later. Even though the intake system and turbo plumbing were completely hand-built and contain many one-off components, the final installation has a factory look to it. This car almost got through the decision cycle before cost and emissions-certification considerations finally killed it. It may have been just as well because the Cobra came along and boosted the car's image at a much lower cost. SUPER FORD *magazine*

1990. There was an official celebration at Griffith Park in Los Angeles on April 17, 1989, that served as the Mustang's 25th birthday party, but any recognition in the model line-up waited until 1990. But 1989 didn't slip away without one other significant occurrence: A small group within Ford was assembled to begin work on the next-generation Mustang, which would come to market five years down the road.

The 1990 Mustangs were again basically unchanged, but there were some minor enhancements and the appearance of a vestigial 25th Anniversary model. The V-8-powered cars did away with the silly 85-mile-per-hour speedometer (a speed the cars could easily break in third gear). Now in place were more appropriate 140-mile-per-hour units. The 5.0 also got a mildly recalibrated camshaft profile, but there was no noticeable difference in performance. Leather upholstery was now an option on GT and LX 5.0 Sport Mustangs and looked especially luxurious on convertible models. All Mustangs carried a small "running horse" badge on the dash that said "25th Anniversary."

When a 25th Anniversary Mustang finally did make the line-up, there were no 351s or twin-turbos to be found. But Ford did put together an attractive package that sold better than originally anticipated. The basic car was a 5.0 Sport convertible, painted Emerald Green metallic and trimmed with a white leather interior and white top. It too carried the 25th Anniversary badge on the dash and got the spoked alloy wheels from the GT. It was available with the buyer's choice of stick shift or automatic. Fortunately, there were no garish anniversary strips or other superfluous bolt-ons; the look was very upmarket. A run of 2,000 of these cars was planned, and 3,837 were ultimately built; they still look good today.

Subtle changes were added to the 1991 models as the 1994 Mustang was already on the drawing boards. The Mustang platform was 13 years old, but Ford kept it fresh with a few worthy upgrades. The LX's handsome wheels dated back to 1985, and the GT wheel design, while newer, also remained a 15-incher. Both cars got new star-shaped five-spoke alloy wheels for 1991. And finally, they made it to 16 inches in diameter. Though still 7 inches wide, the new wheel allowed the mounting of 225/55 ZR-16 tires. The shorter sidewall made for crisper steering and more road feel at the expense of just a small bit of ride quality. Goodyear and Michelin tires were used, and the new rolling stock package was a much-welcomed improvement.

The 1991 Mustangs also received a driver's-side airbag. No airbag was fitted on the passenger side as that would have necessitated a redesign of the dash, not a cost-effective move with a new Mustang just a few years up the road. No other big news, unless you count the side pinstripe now being a delete option. The most unfortu-

nate aspect of the 1991 model year was sagging sales. After slipping to 128,189 cars for 1990, sales fell again for 1991 to just 98,737. This was the first time in several years that sales dipped below the 100,000 mark. The Fox-platformed Mustang was getting old, and the market continued to pummel it with new, slick-handling offerings. None were as reasonably priced as the Mustang, especially in LX form, and darn few packed 225 horses.

The motto for 1992 could have been "as carryover as carryover could be." Other than a red-and-white version of the 1989 Anniversary special, there was nothing else to talk about. It should have been no surprise that sales continued to dwindle, just 79,280 Mustangs left dealers lots.

It was clear that after nearly 15 years, it was time for a new Mustang. However, the Fox-platform Mustang certainly went out in style in 1993. Besides the formation of SVT (Ford's Special Vehicle Team—see chapter 6) in late 1991 and the 1993 SVT Cobra version of the Mustang, there were a couple of final special-edition mainstream offerings. Again sticking to the monochromatic theme, Ford offered an eye-popping yellow-over-white LX convertible with chrome 16-inch wheels and a "Palm Springs Special" (our words, not Ford's) all-white combo. This convert had a white exterior, white leather interior, a white top, and even white-painted alloy wheels. About 1,400 of each were sold as part of a rebound year for Mustang. Sales increased a bit, ending up at 114,228 cars.

One other interesting bit of number news concerned the 5.0's horsepower rating. It had been rated at 225 horsepower since its 1987 remodel. Yet without changing any hardware, Ford lowered the horsepower number to 205 for 1993 only. The engine didn't just lose horsepower; Ford's official line was that the method by which it rated horsepower had been changed and that this was really a more accurate number.

A few friends of mine within Ford hint this move was really a marketing ploy. As you'll see, the new-for-1994 Mustang would retain the OHC, 5.0 V-8, and it would be rated at 215 horsepower. The rumble is that the marketing types could not fathom a new car hitting the market with 10 less horsepower than the old favorite, so the number was artificially lowered for 1993, so it could be raised again for the new car.

True? Ford says "no way." Hard to say, but stranger things have happened in the car business.

The Fox-platform served longer than anyone dreamed it would have, and there was a faction that recognized its performance-per-dollar quotient and never wanted it to change. But a new Camaro hit the street in 1993 with swoopy looks, a 275-horse V-8, six-speed manual transmission, and improved handling. Thankfully, a new Mustang was on the boards and coming for 1994.

# *four* Call Me SN

The Fox-bodied Mustang served ably, but its day as a market-competitive product had come and gone. Few expected it would last the 15 model years that it did. The 1993 SVT Cobra gave the old Fox a rousing send off, but ergonomics needed modernization, the chassis needed improvement, and the market demanded fresh styling.

A new chassis for the Mustang was of paramount importance. Racing, the aftermarket, and computer-aided design had taught carmakers that a rigid, torsionally stiff chassis is the key to building a solid automobile with good handling characteristics. The principle is much the same as constructing a building: If the foundation is solid, the building will be stable. If the foundation is unstable or shaky in any way, the resulting structure will be too, no matter how well the upper part of the building is constructed.

If a car's chassis is torsionally rigid (not to be confused with a "stiff" suspension with ultra-hard springs and shocks), then the suspension can be tuned with much greater precision. A rigid chassis means less variation in caster, camber, and toe as a car powers through turns and less hopping around when a bump is encountered in the middle of that turn. Finally, it allows a better compromise between ride and handling, because if the chassis is not flexing, softer springs and shocks can be specified to preserve ride quality.

The 1994 GTs, coupe, and convertible. This coupe has the optional 17-inch wheels first seen on the 1993 Cobra R, while the convertible wears the standard 16-inch wheels. The restyling job, the first new bodywork in 15 years, was generally well received, with the possible exception of the horizontal taillights, which really didn't resemble those of the original Mustang. They would be revised just two years later. Note the reappearance of the running horse in the grille opening. *Ford Motor Company publicity photo*

The design and marketing teams which worked on the 1994 Mustang project made certain the car had strong ties to the original Mustangs. The final result indicates both teams were successful. This Ford public relations photo places the 1994 Mustang with a Mustang from each of the previous generations. Note that all the cars in this photo are fastbacks, except the Mustang II. *Ford Motor Company publicity photo*

By early 1990s standards, the Fox's unit body chassis had too much flex. Aftermarket companies had developed several chassis-stiffening devices in an attempt to minimize this condition and were successful to a large degree. Budgetary constraints did not allow a from-scratch platform, as a rear-wheel-drive sporty car chassis was not likely to be used to create an entire line-up of vehicles. Ford was already at work on another world car platform, the Ford Mondeo, which came to American markets as the Ford Contour and the Mercury Mystique. The Mondeo/Contour/Mystique chassis is a more versatile four-door, front-wheel-drive platform. So given the limited uses of a rear-wheel-drive coupe platform, it was decided the new Mustang would stem from an extensively revised

Fox chassis. The go-ahead to build a new Mustang was given in the fall of 1991, and the new platform was dubbed FOX-4. The terminology "FOX" was taken from the prior chassis name but changed to all capitals, and "4" indicated the year the program would debut—1994.

Fortunately, Ford learned a bit of a lesson during the Probe episode.

According to Janine Bay, Mustang chief project engineer, "We have since come to the strong realization that there is a strong difference between that customer body [for front-wheel-drive sporty coupes] and the customer body of what we call 'pony cars.' It was a very helpful revelation . . . there is room for coexistence for those two types of products in the marketplace."

This early conceptual drawing evolved into the Arnold Schwarzenegger concept car that evolved into the new Mustang. The forward cut of the C-pillar, the "C" scoop down the side of the car, and the round simulated air intakes on the hood were already in place. This dual-exhaust treatment may have been quite attractive had it made production. The date on this rendering is 10/91. *Ford Motor Company publicity photo*

Looking like a cross between an NHRA Funny Car and a small spaceship, the Rambo concept car was judged too aggressive for most tastes. A close look at that front end shows a startling resemblance to the new-for-1993 Pontiac Firebird. Another interesting aspect of this rendering is the 4.0-liter engine size that is noted on the hood. Was there a 4.0-liter engine under development at the same time? *Ford Motor Company publicity photo*

The Bruce Jenner concept car was judged a bit too soft for Mustang enthusiasts. This is an extremely early full-sized rendering, dated 11/6/89, not long after the SN-95 Mustang design team was assembled. *Ford Motor Company publicity photo*

This SN-95 chassis display model demonstrates some of the areas where the platform received attention. The red pieces were all new, the yellow pieces were new but for convertibles only, and the white indicated carryover pieces from the 1993-and-earlier Fox platform. The green strut-tower brace—just visible over the engine bay—shows one of the efforts taken to stiffen the platform. The brace was an idea originated by aftermarket car builder Kenny Brown. *Ford Motor Company publicity photo*

David Kimball is the master of automotive cutaway art. Ford commissioned him to draw the 1994 Mustang GT coupe. *Ford Motor Company publicity photo*

Though vestigial elements of the original Fox remained, it was essentially a new car. True to form, it retained rear-wheel drive, MacPherson strut suspension up front, a live axle out back, and an engine up front, but that was about it. The new Mustang would occupy about the same amount of driveway space as the old, but dimensions were slightly increased all around: Wheelbase was up .8 inch (111.3 versus 110.5), and overall length increased about 2 inches. FOX-4 was also about 2 inches wider, an inch taller (53.1 versus 52.1), and the track increased between 1 and 2 inches as well.

To increase chassis stiffness—and provide better ride and improved, more consistent handling—the FOX-4 received many new chassis components and a

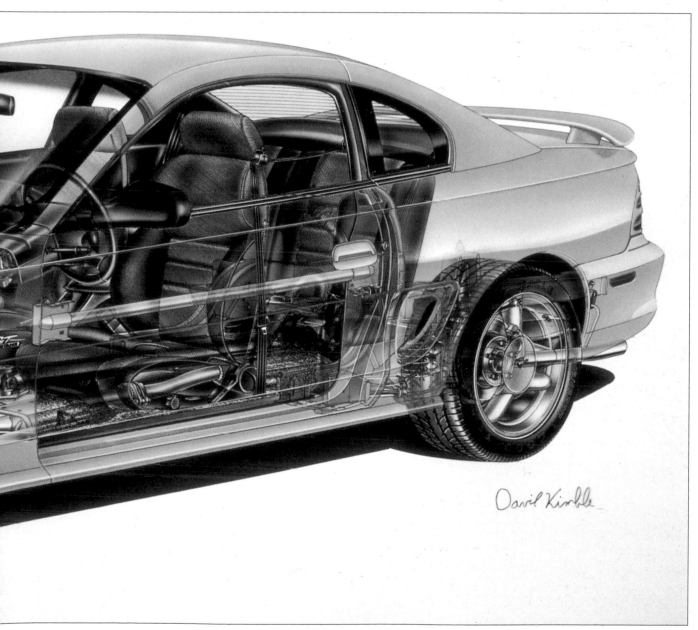

Mustang's new interior was a hit. The dual-pod cockpit flavor was a blending of modern and retro, though it may seem a bit more reminiscent of Corvette than Mustang. It was also a neat way to incorporate the dual airbags. Ergonomics were greatly improved, and the Mach 460 stereo system provides terrific tunes. The only complaint was limited seat-travel and a shortage of leg room for taller drivers. *Ford Motor Company*

change in body configurations. "It is very difficult, if not impossible, to build a torsionally stiff three-door hatchback," commented Will Boddie, director of Small and Midsize Car Segment. Because the hatchback has a large opening in the back of the body to accommodate the liftgate, the Mustang body-style line-up was going to be reconciled from three to two.

The closed car would be a cross between the Fox's notchback and hatchback: a fastback-styled car, not as upright as the previous notchback but retaining a formal trunk. The structure around the trunk area, as well as a coupe roofline, would allow the stiff chassis the Mustang team was after. The other body style would be a convertible, designed from the ground up this time, and also built in-house by Ford.

The underbody reveals a redesigned floor-pan, a revised front cross-member, and an X-brace stiffening structure placed just below the engine oil pan. The front suspension remains a MacPherson strut unit, though the geometry and mounting points were revised: The front cross-member was moved forward, and the control arms

were made slightly longer. Larger box sections in the roof rails and rocker panels strengthened the basic body-in-white, with better-gusseted joints boosting rigidity as well. The results were worth the effort. The 1994 coupe body, for example, is 56 percent stiffer in bending and 44 percent stiffer in torsion than the design it replaced.

Styling of any new car is critical, but for one that sells itself on a performance image—and for a car with nearly 30 years of history—the look of the new Mustang could literally make it or break it. The small groups charged in 1989 with coming up with the makeup of the new Mustang went to the logical place: the DNA of the originals. The trick was how to blend the image that the Fox-bodied cars

The Bob Bondurant School of High Performance Driving uses Ford products exclusively for all its courses and demonstrations. While there are a few LTDs, Taurus SHOs, and Fox Mustangs at the Arizona-based facility, most of the fleet consists of new SN-95 Mustangs—approximately 100 in total. *Matt Stone*

had developed, heritage from the original cars (considered to be vitally important), and new shapes and styling cues to take the car into the 1990s. To gain insights, they held consumer clinics and focus-group activities around the country throughout the later part of 1989 and early 1990. Mustang club members, magazine editors, dealers, and potential new car buyers gave their opinions. These Mustang clinics were colloquially named "the gallop poles."

Early Mustang cues were important, so said the people. "Bring back the galloping horse" was heard time and again, as well as the C-shape scoops between the rear edge of the door and the front edge of the rear wheelwell. As the information was assimilated, the design team—led by Mustang Design Manager Bud Magaldi—assembled story boards like those used by animators in the rough development stage of an animated motion picture.

As the project really got rolling in 1990, Magaldi's team began to work on three different proposals. Though all three were similar in terms of basic form and proportion, they were served somewhat like salsa: mild, medium, and spicy. The team named them according to an image they believed each projected. The smoothest yet still muscular design was dubbed "Bruce Jenner." "It had a very nice, modern look," according to Magaldi. "But its overall shapes were too smooth, too clean and friendly, too nice" to be a Mustang. More spice please.

At the opposite end of the spectrum was "Rambo." The Rambo design, like its movie namesake, bristled with machismo at every turn. The headlights practically glinted, the front spoiler jutted like Stallone's lower jaw, and the scoops and character lines were deeply creased. A little too aggressive, thank you.

Much like Baby Bear's porridge, the "Arnold Schwarzenegger" design was judged to be just right. Even in its earliest configurations, the 1994 Mustang can be clearly seen, save for a few details. And the C-scoop and running pony were right where they belong. There were other styling elements that obviously came from previous Mustangs, such as the reverse-slant of the C-pillar and the three-element taillights. Those new rear

Saleen uses this innovative "plastic man" display to show off the look of the factory-optional removable hardtop. *Matt Stone*

lights got a twist, however, literally 90 degrees, and ran horizontally rather than vertically, as they did on the 1964-1/2 through 1973 models. "Arnold" got preliminary approval in late 1990 and final senior-management approval in September 1991. Ford's "World Class Timing" approach to the car's development mandated it be done in just 35 months for a Job One rollout date of October 1994, as opposed to the more common 42- and 48-month product development cycles. Budget for the Mustang's remodel, officially dubbed SN-95, was $700 million, relatively inexpensive in a world of $2-billion platform-development projects.

One of the main areas of the Mustang needing attention was brakes. The Fox car carried four-wheel disc brakes twice in its production lifetime: from 1984–1986 on the SVO and on the 1993 SVT Cobra. But both of these were limited-edition models; Z-28s had them as standard equipment for years. Budget restrictions were the likely reasons that kept drum brakes on the rear ends of 140-mile-per-hour, 225-horsepower Mustangs for years, a big mistake but one that would finally be corrected.

The new car got beefy, power, four-wheel disc brakes at all four corners: 10.5 inches out back and 10.8 inches in front, and the front units were also vented. For those who wanted anti-lock braking, it was offered as an option for the first time. Finally the Mustang would have the "whoa" to go with the "go." Along with this revision came the switch to five-lug hubs.

Inside, there was little to be recognized from the previous Mustang other than the shift knob and galloping horse logo; the balance of the cabin was redone from scratch. In the interest of recalling past themes, the new interior was designed around a dual-cockpit theme. "I researched the entire history of Mustang interior design, beginning with the original car, and we incorporated a lot of the historical features, such as the double-pod cockpit theme," commented Emeline King, one of the interior designers on the Team Mustang. "We also focused on good ergonomics—

There were numerous assembly workers and other Ford employees who had the opportunity to work on both the 1964-1/2 and 1994 Mustangs. Here is one such group, photographed at the Mustang's Dearborn assembly plant. *Ford Motor Company*

such as locating the radio up high so you could reach it easier [than on the previous models, where it was behind the shifter]. The entire upper area of the dashboard has been darkened to cut down on glare."

The look is certainly exciting, though not everyone warmed to the two-tone dash (in the case of a car with something other than a black interior). The new fascia also neatly incorporated dual airbags, another first for Mustang, and something that most of the market had come around to by 1994. Another interesting feature was the little blister-shaped nacelle that held the clock and was positioned in the middle of the dash. Some like it, as it recalls the dual-pod dash; others hate it, saying it looks like an afterthought. Another common complaint heard from taller drivers was a lack of front-seat travel.

Though not perfect, most agree it's an exceptional design, one that still looks good today as the SN-95 Mustang enters its fifth year in production. Besides recalling the flavor of the 1969–1970 Mach I, it also brings to mind the late 1950s and early 1960s Corvettes, particularly in the interior. And nobody complained about the optional Mach 460 sound system with

its 460 watts of power, eight-element speaker system, and optional, built-in CD player. It's clearly the best sound system ever offered in a Mustang.

The engine/trim packaging was completely overhauled. As with the previous notchback and LX versions, the four-cylinder base iteration was also history. In its place, a new V-6-motivated Mustang served as the base offering. And to the chagrin of LX 5.0 Sport fans, all V-8-powered cars were now GTs. So the line-up simply consisted of base V-6- and V-8-powered GTs, in either coupe or convertible form. Easy enough.

The new V-6 was certainly a smart move on Ford's part, as the 2.3-liter, Lima four-cylinder engine dated back 20 years to the day of the first Mustang II and was neither particularly smooth nor powerful. It would not be missed, and there was no four-cylinder Camaro counterpart, so why bother? In its place was the 3.8-liter Vulcan V-6, which had been doing duty in a number of Ford products, such as the Taurus and Thunderbird. The Vulcan was a 145-horsepower OHV unit and could be mated with either a five-speed manual transmission or the four-speed automatic overdrive unit. Though not

# Mustang Mach III Show Car

Concept cars, or "dream" cars as they are often colloquially referred to, accomplish a lot for a manufacturer. They can help an automaker gauge market response to a certain look or vehicle concept. They can also give the buying public a hint of what may be coming down the pike in order to build or maintain interest in the new product until it arrives. Concept cars work as public relations tools, hopefully garnering their share of ink and magazine covers. Occasionally, in cases such as the Dodge Viper, they can captivate the public to the point where the manufacturer ends up building a car they never intended to in the first place.

In early 1992 it was common knowledge that a new Mustang was on its way, and Ford elected to tease the public and media about it in the form of a dazzling show car called the Mach III. It was put together by Team Mustang to give everyone an idea of what the new-for-1994 Mustang would look like without really showing it. There were two Mach III's built, both identical orange cars that were two-seater roadsters in the purest sense. This concept harks back to the very original Mustang I prototype; it too was a two-seat roadster, though a mid-engined one.

The 1994 Mustang's presence is obvious in the frontal aspect (including the all-important running horse in the grille area), in the rear taillights, and in the dual-pod cockpit interior, though, as usual, the themes were taken to an extreme for show car purposes. The look was extremely modern and clearly retro at the same time. Modernity was expressed in elements like carbon-fiber trim and the hand-built 19-inch wheels. Yet look inside, and the wood-and-mahogany steering wheel and round, white-faced gauges could have come from any high-dollar roadster of the 1950s . . . with just

CONTINUED ON PAGE 60

*Just a glance at the Mustang Mach III concept car indicates where the new Mustang was headed stylistically. Though this car was a pure roadster with no top, many SN-95 Mustang styling cues were present, especially in the frontal aspect. The unique wheels were black steel with a handmade, chromed plastic insert. It's a shame that the Mach III's supercharged 450-horsepower, 4.6-liter modular V-8 engine never made it into a production Mustang. The Mach III toured the show-car circuit in early 1993. Matt Stone*

a little bit of a Shelby Mustang ring to them. The interior was finished in an especially attractive nappy blue suede, and even the upcoming "blister" clock nacelle was located up on the dash.

While many such concept cars are "pushmobiles," meaning they have no drivetrain and need to be pushed everywhere, that was not the case with the Mach III. If anything, it had the drivetrain everyone wished would have appeared in some sort of high-line Mustang, a 4.6-liter double-overhead-cam V-8 borrowed from the upcoming Lincoln Mark VIII. But in this case, it was replete with a supercharger and intercoolers. The modular 4.6 was rated at 280 horsepower in the Mark but put out an estimated 450 horses with the hand-built blower system. It was mated to a five-speed manual transmission and a standard Mustang rear end.

I remember seeing the car at the Los Angeles Auto Show during its media unveiling in January 1992. After the presentation, the staff hopped in, fired it up, and drove it around the show floor. I'll never forget the crisp bark of the 4.6, and each of us hoped that an engine of this type would make it into the Mustang at some point or another. We also had the chance to watch a video of the car being tested, and believe me, it was no pushmobile. The tape showed the Mach III simply melting its rear tires into a cloud of smoke all the way through first and second gear.

As the Viper came to market for 1992, there was considerable pressure on Ford to respond by making a production version of the Mach III as a performance flagship to sell alongside the upcoming Mustang. But Ford had no intent of doing so, and the Mach III remained an exceptionally interesting show car . . . and a hint of Mustangs soon to come.

*The new Mustang's dual-pod interior theme was demonstrated by Mach III, even down to the newly styled "Mustang" script. Several other of its design elements showed up in other Ford models: the white-faced gauges appeared on the SVT Cobra Mustang, and the oval-shaped panel holding many of the car's ancillary controls would later show up on the new-for-1996 Ford Taurus. Too bad the wood steering wheel had to go . . . Matt Stone*

intended as a performance application, the V-6 offered decent torque, good fuel economy, and at least a bit of enjoyment potential when combined with the five-speed.

The Mustang everyone had waited for was the V-8-powered GT. For SN-95's first two years on the market, the engine offering was the tried-and-true, 5.0-liter V-8, now rated at 215 horsepower. It was much the same as it was in the Fox-bodied GT and LX 5.0 of 1993 and earlier, except it borrowed the intake system from the 5.0-liter-powered Thunderbird. The reason for the intake-system change was the Mustang's lower frontal aspect and hoodline; the previous, and slightly taller, Mustang intake system did not fit. The GT also picked up a bit more chassis stiffness in the form of a strut-tower brace, a tubular bar that triangulated the shock towers and firewall. Where did Ford come up with this idea? From the aftermarket, where companies had been making them for Fox-bodied cars for years.

The whole horsepower issue is a bit funny for at least two reasons. One was the 215-horsepower rating itself. When fitted to the Thunderbird with a slightly different camshaft, the engine was good for 200 horsepower. When fitted to the 1993 Mustang with the taller and supposedly better-breathing intake, it was rated at 205 horsepower. So how did it produce 215 horsepower in the new Mustang?

A bigger question, and one that still plagues Ford and the Mustang is: How could Ford let Chevrolet trump them with the Camaro? When Chevrolet debuted an all-new Camaro for 1993, they powered it with a slightly detuned version of the Corvette's LT1 350-cubic-inch V-8. It was rated at 275 horsepower, was backed by a Borg-Warner six-speed transmission, and went like a banshee. Ford had to know this was coming, though the Mustang program was likely well down the road by the time Ford found out that the Camaro was about to get serious horsepower for 1993. Ford had a more powerful engine ready, the 240-horse version out of the SVT Cobra (see chapter 6). So why didn't they use it?

They couldn't as that would have left no "up step" powerplant for the new Cobra. Besides, Ford believed the new car would be enough of a change and a success to notch the necessary sales. In that respect they were correct. But the performance bragging rights were handed over to Chevrolet on a silver platter, much to the chagrin of Mustang loyals who were hoping for something to compete with those nasty bow-tie machines.

As with the V-6, there were two transmission offerings for the 5.0: a Borg-Warner T-5 five-speed manual or Ford's excellent four-speed automatic overdrive gearbox. Why no six-speed? Ford's contention is that with the 5.0's excellent torque curve and driveability, the six-speed is really just a marketing bragging right and would not improve performance by any measurable amount. Bragging rights maybe, but isn't image part of what these cars are all about? In practice, however, the five-speed worked as fine in the new car as it did in the old.

Ford did go GM one better in the wheel and tire department, however. The GT got a revised version of the 1991–1993 five-spoke alloy as its standard equipment, retaining both the 7x16-inch size, and the 225/55ZR16 tire sizing. But optional was a new 17-inch package, upping the ante with a 245/45ZR17 Goodyear Eagle GSC tire package. Chevy and Pontiac only had 16-inchers at the time (though an optional 17-inch wheel would follow a few years later). This rolling stock upgrade enhanced the Mustang's cornering ability, raising its breakaway limits, and further sharpening the steering response. The wheel style was another one of those "love it or hate it" affairs. The aftermarket had been pushing three-spoke wheel designs for a few years as a trendy, futuristic look. The Mustang's "triple-twin" spoke look was modern, but not a stylistic success to some. But at least they were finally the right size to give the chassis some bite, though handling was also enhanced due to a nearly 20-percent increase in roll stiffness via the recalibrated suspension.

There were a few interesting aspects to the convertible design. One was the tonneau cover, which is a neat, easy-to-install, three-piece plastic affair. Once in place, it covers the entire top, making a neat, finished appearance. The SN-95 is rather tall at the back end, but at least the stack-height of the top when closed is flush with the back deck. Ford also developed a one-piece, fiberglass top, à la Mercedes SL, which could be used to transform a "convertible" into a coupe. The only problem was that it was heavy, required two people to install, took up a considerable amount of storage space, and was rather pricey at about $1,000. The top didn't appear until 1995; precious few were sold (499), mostly on SVT Cobras; and the option was dropped—certainly already a collectible piece!

Though there will always be a cadre of loyalists who like the Fox cars better (a good thing in that it maintains interest, value, and aftermarket involvement in the older cars), it would be hard to say the new Mustang wasn't a better car in most ways. It handled better, stopped much better, enjoyed a vastly improved interior, and went just about as well. Depending upon which magazine you read and who was driving on test day, acceleration times were just about the same as they were for the last Fox 5.0s. Weight was up about 100 pounds, depending upon model and equipment (the 10 speakers in a Mach 460 sound system probably weighed that much alone).

Overall, the media's response to the new car was positive. *Road & Track* reported, "The GTs have always gripped well through corners, as long as the road was glassy-smooth. Throw a couple of lumps or frost heaves into that corner, however, and things in the old car could get exciting pretty fast. Where the 1993 Mustang got distinctly frisky on bumpy corners, the new car is noticeably more composed. Only a combination of speed, braking, and washboard surface brings out the GT's live axle stutter."

Though *R & T's* editors emphasized the 60-horsepower deficiency compared to the GM F-bodies, they felt that the new Mustang still captured the correct spirit of the car and believed the improvements were worth the effort. "But those diehards with the 'Friends don't let friends drive Chevys' T-shirts can still rejoice in the reworked Mustang," they said. "If they're uncomfortable with the car's softer styling and refined demeanor, they can rest assured; it's this shift in emphasis that makes the new Mustang so much better than the old. Where the old car got by on its kick-butt, straight-line performance, the new car provides a much more entertaining, better rounded package. And if some people lament the change in focus, they'll only regret it up to the first corner."

What some people did regret, however, was a fairly substantial increase in price. Granted, costs go up over time. The development cost of any new car needs to be amortized, and the new Mustang had content levels the old one could only dream about. But it all came at a price: the GT coupe increased about $1,500 ($15,850 versus $17,280), and there was no lower-cost LX 5.0 version. GT convertibles now based at $21,970. Touch every option box on the convertible's order form, and you created the first $25,000 Mustang. Now it's not that Mustang didn't provide value for those dollars, but there was a rub: Identically equipped cars actually cost anywhere from $500 to $1,000 more than an equal Z-28. Pretty hard to reconcile given the whopping 60-horsepower deficit.

It mattered little. Chalk it up to the new design and an extremely high level of brand loyalty—hey, this is the Mustang we're talking about here—and the market responded with sales of 137,074 cars. This represented an increase of about 15 percent and a substantial improvement over the 80,000 figure posted just two years earlier. It also beat out the numbers for Camaro and Firebird *combined*, so it's obvious that horsepower ratings aren't everything.

Considering how new the car was for 1994, it was only reasonable to expect little change for 1995. But Ford did attempt to satiate those who missed the simplicity, lighter weight, and lower cost of the previous LX 5.0 Sport model. In mid-1995, and with little fanfare, the Mustang GTS model joined the line-up. It was a de-contented GT and an honest effort to recall the LX flavor. The GTS still packed the 215-horsepower V-8 and all the GT's suspension underpinnings but gave up the front fog lights, rear wing, power locks, windows, and power driver's seat. Power mirrors

stayed, as that was the only design Ford offered. There was no special GTS identification; about the only way to tell the difference was that the fog lamps and spoiler were not in place. The sticker price came down about $2,000, and though it never really took off with the mainstream-buying public, it was popular with those who bought a Mustang for racing purposes or with the intent to highly modify it anyway. With more than 185,000 cars sold, the 1995 Mustang turned out to be the most popular model of the decade, again proof-positive that there was life in the old horse yet.

Though the Mustang has never related to any animal other than a horse, it could in some ways be analogous to a cat in that it seems to have many lives and keeps coming back. The "Mazstang"/Probe situation almost spelled the end for the V-8-powered, rear-wheel-drive car in the mid-1980s. There were also factions within Ford that would have let it die quietly at the end of 1993, the year a new and more powerful V-6-powered Probe came out. But fortunately the "good guys won," and SN-95 did indeed see the light of day. But to keep it fresh and technologically moving forward toward the end of the century, more changes were needed. For 1996, they would, this time, be found under the hood.

It didn't take SVE boss John Coletti long to whip up a special concept car to show the media and the show-car circuit what could be done with the new Mustang. Coletti's gang tossed out the 5.0-liter in favor of an old favorite, the hemi-head 429 "Shotgun" motor. Actually, it's a Boss only in design; the block and heads are aftermarket pieces cast by AR, and with a stroker crank, the engine measures 604 cubic inches. But running a passel of Holley 735s would have been a bit too retro-tech, so a special fuel-injection system was hand-fabricated. The engine was backed by a heavily modified Ford C-6 three-speed automatic, and horsepower estimates ranged from 670 to 750. The Boss stripe and paint theme were no accident as this engine's last street-version appearance was in the Boss 429 of 1970. And this car was no "trailer queen." It had quarter-mile times in the mid-10-second range, and Coletti was not shy about taking it out "cruising" on the streets of Detroit to gauge reaction from the local Mustang (and Chevrolet) crowd. SUPER FORD *magazine*

# *five* Good-Bye 5.

# 0, Hello 4.6
## 1996-1998 AND BEYOND

The original small-block "Fairlane" Ford V-8 that fathered the current 5.0-liter engine had been around since 1961. Originally offered in 221- and 260-cubic-inch form—with horsepower that wouldn't impress a Honda VTEC—the original V-8 was exceptionally small, light, and powerful for its time. It had served Ford well, having powered everything from Cobras to pickup trucks, Indy winners, and grocery-getters. But Ford, like many other manufacturers, sensed that the days of the cast-iron, pushrod V-8 were numbered (sad, though it may seem). This is not to say the world would be satisfied with four-bangers and V-6s, but a new family of V-8s would be necessary to meet world platform needs, ever tightening emissions and fuel-economy requirements, revised production methods, and a myriad of other issues facing a large car maker.

The answer to this question, and likely to many others in the future, was a new family of engines. We say "family" because the days of tooling up for unique engine lines were no longer cost effective either. Ford was more guilty of this than anyone. In 1970, for example, Ford offered four different V-8 engine designs: the FE (390/427/428 cubic inches), the 385 (429/460), the

The badge says it all. The 5.0 era that began in 1979 and took a few years off in 1980 and 1981 made a permanent exit in 1996. Interestingly enough, the same chrome "5.0" badge was used throughout all those years. The "GT 4.6L" badge signified that the overhead-cam era had arrived. *Matt Stone*

From a front three-quarters angle, it's difficult to distinguish a 1996–1998 car from a 1994–1995. The honeycombed plastic grille that appeared for 1996 was already gone by 1997.-*Matt Stone*

65

The visual differences for 1996 are certainly noticeable from the rear angle—note the 17-inch wheels and the revised three-element taillights. Most agree that the new taillight design was an improvement, and as the lenses are now vertically oriented, they become a much better representation of the original 1964-1/2 through 1973 design. The light housings themselves have a dimpled reflector surface, giving a bit of a jewel-like effect when the lights are on. Note that the very lower portion of the rear bumper, which had been painted black on the 1994–1995 Mustangs, is now body color on this 1997 GT. *Matt Stone*

Cleveland (351), and the Windsor (302/351). Chevrolet covered the same gamut of horsepower and cubic-inch offerings with two engine-block designs.

Ford conceived of a "modular" engine design, one that could easily and cost effectively spawn engines of different size and cylinder count while still making use of the same basic design, layout, and architecture. There was current and future need for V-8s and V-6s, but there would be increasing need for inline fours, perhaps even V-4s and maybe, someday, V-10s and V-12s.

The first designs to be built at Ford's Romeo, Michigan, engine plant and thus colloquially dubbed the Romeo modular engine family were V-8s of 4.6 liters (281 cubic inches). The new SOHC cam V-8 was designed and built to engineering levels not possible when the original 221 Fairlane small-block came out in the early 1960s. The cast-iron engine block was much stronger and stiffer than the old 5.0, and the cylinder heads were cast in alloy.

Engine accessories (alternator, power steering pump, air conditioning compressor) were bolted directly to the engine, saving the weight of accessory brackets, and reducing noise, vibration, and harshness. Metallurgy had certainly come a long way since the JFK presidency, and the new Romeo used materials designed around tighter production tolerances and longer engine life. Surprisingly, the engine does not have exhaust headers in the classic sense. It returns to a cast-iron exhaust manifold that flows at least as well as the tube headers found on the old 5.0. The engine also had 6-quart oiling, distributorless ignition, cross-bolted main-bearing caps, direct-port fuel injection, and Ford's newest EEC-V engine control system. The list goes on, but suffice it to say, the new V-8 was a technical tour de force, for sure.

The Romeo V-8 debuted in the two-valve per cylinder form in the 1991 Lincoln Town Car and appeared in the revised Ford Crown Victoria and Mercury Grand Marquis the following year. If it was already available, why didn't it also show up in the new-for-1994 Mustang? "There were several reasons," according to Janine Bay, Mustang chief program engineer. "At first, we didn't have the production capacity at Romeo for the new engines." Could it also have been that Ford didn't want to alienate the 5.0 traditionalist with both a new engine and a new body style at the same time? "Absolutely true," according to Bay. It's also common for a manufacturer to bring out new hardware in the highest price lines first.

For 1996 it was finally time for new-tech Romeo powerplants to make their appearance in the Mustang, and appear they did. Replacing the old 5.0 in the GT was a 4.6-liter, 215-horsepower version of the SOHC cam modular V-8. The real performance news for 1996 came in the form of a double-overhead-cam, four-valve-per-cylinder, all-alloy V-8 for the SVT Cobra. This 305-horsepower stormer will be liberally discussed in chapter 6, so we'll restrict the balance of this chapter to the GT version.

Note that the horsepower rating of the new engine is identical to the old 5.0. Was this a design goal, a coincidence, or the number being somewhat driven by a marketing need? Recall that the 1987–1992 Mustangs were rated at 225 horses, then the number was "adjusted" to 205 even though no changes were made to the engine. For 1994 the engine was uprated to 215 horsepower even though it had a more restrictive intake system but a larger-diameter exhaust system. One source, who requested anonymity, says the power outputs are really quite close, so it's certainly not a total image-making move, but Ford's marketing folk still decreed the output number for the new Mustang engine would be at least 215 . . . no matter what it was. The old-guard 5.0-liter enthusiasts would laugh all the way to the drag strip if it wasn't. Truth or rumor? "Not a chance," according to Jim Clarke, one of Ford Powertrain's chief engineers. "We do not manipulate those types of numbers and ratings."

As noted, the single-overhead-cam V-8 utilized a two-valves-per-cylinder layout, maintaining good air velocity into the head and offering decent low-end torque, a point of criticism with many overhead-cam engines. Backing the new V-8 was a choice of two new transmissions: Borg Warner's new T-45 five-speed manual or a Ford 4R70W four-speed electronically controlled automatic. Though the T-45 stems from the same design as the previous T-5, its gears are manufactured via an improved process that allows for quieter running and an increased torque rating. The new automatic offered crisper performance and smoother shifting than the autobox it replaced.

Several improvements were brought on line in 1996. The SN-95 Mustang's taillights had been the subject of controversy since the car's introduction. In short,

The new 4.6-liter OHC V-8 is a neat fit. Note the high center-mounting of the alternator and dual cam-driven distributors. Compare this to the older engine compartments, and you'll see how Ford takes much greater care with details such as material selection, finishes, and how the wiring is run and tied down. The triangle-shaped engine-bay brace reduces chassis flex. It was invented in the aftermarket, but Ford developed it into a factory-fitted component for the SN-95 Mustang. *Matt Stone*

many thought they were ugly. And even though they were of a three-element design, supposedly to recall the look of the original Mustang's lights, the light bars ran horizontally, as opposed to vertically (so much for tradition). In any case, a new taillight cluster showed up for 1996 that more accurately, and much more handsomely, replicated the vertical bar look. Furthermore, the new lenses had a diamond-effect reflector, adding a somewhat jewel-like quality to the lights. Much better.

While the GT's base 16-inch, five-spoke alloy wheels were handsome enough, the triple-twin spoke 17-incher was never well received. Ford's wheel design group came up with a new modern interpretation on the five-spoke theme that was offered in either silver-painted or diamond-cut and clearcoated finish. The last visual change was a bit hard to notice, though it too recalled Mustangs of an earlier day. The 1994–1995 Mustang had no grille covering the air intake (just the floating horse), but the 1996 model carried a black grille, the surface of which is hexagonal grating . . . just like a 1964 1/2.

With the SN-95 Mustang being just two years old, one would have thought that the above noted new engines and appearance revisions would have been enough, but credit Ford for acting upon what it learned

# It's Still Ford versus Chevy (and Pontiac)

To the automotive enthusiast, particularly of the American V-8 variety, horsepower numbers and 0–60 times are still the bragging rights of choice. Ford and GM have volleyed the lead in these categories back and forth many times over the years. Even though there are other factors that affect a car's net accelerative performance (such as the car's weight, the transmission type, and the engine's torque curve), horsepower is still the magic ingredient that grabs everyone's attention. Here's a look at how those volleys have gone over the years. The horsepower ratings shown are for the top offerings in the marketplace by year with special models noted accordingly. Turbocharged, V-6, and other configurations are not shown; these numbers are for V-8 models only:

| Model Year | Mustang | Camaro / Firebird |
|---|---|---|
| 1979 | 140 | 185 |
| 1980 | 119 | 185 |
| 1981 | 120 | 185 |
| 1982 | 157 | 145 |
| 1983 | 175 | 160 |
| 1984 | 175 | 190 |
| 1985 | 210 | 190 |
| 1986 | 200 | 190 |
| 1987 | 225 | 215 |
| 1988 | 225 | 215 |
| 1989 | 225 | 240 |
| 1990 | 225 | 240 |
| 1991 | 225 | 240 |
| 1992 | 215 | 240 |
| 1993 | 240 (Cobra) 205 (GT, LX) | 275 |
| 1994 | 240 (Cobra) 215 (GT) | 275 |
| 1995 | 240 (Cobra) 215 (GT) | 275 |
| 1996 | 305 (Cobra) 215 (GT) | 305 (SS) 285 Z28 |
| 1997 | 305 (Cobra) 215 (GT) | 305 (SS) 285 Z28 |
| 1998 | 305 (Cobra) 225 (GT) | 320 (SS) 305 Z28 |

**Iceman's Triumph:**
**Winston Cup Champ Terry Labonte**
**Ends a 12-year Drought**

# AutoWeek

November 18, 1996
$2.50 USA $3.50 Canada

## POTENT

CAMARO SS

RAM AIR FIREBIRD

## PONIES

MUSTANG COBRA

**AutoFile Special**

*Life with America's premier muscle cars*

The cam covers of the SOHC 4.6-liter V-8 have a finned, black-crinkle finish that recalls the "Powered By Ford" valve covers from the Cobra days. The heads are aluminum alloy, and the crossbolts for the lower mains can be seen in this photo. The cast-iron exhaust manifolds are said to flow as well as steel tube headers. *Ford Motor Company publicity photo*

from those first 1994 Mustang owners. Also new for 1996 was a revised rack and pinion steering system with a bit sharper turn-in and response, especially noticeable on cars with the 17-inch wheel and tire package. The new EEC-V delivered quicker-reacting engine management, and much to the chagrin of many backyard tuners, compliance with new federal On-Board Diagnostics II (OBD II) requirements. Don't forget five new colors.

Besides the steering, there were other chassis revisions. According to Janine Bay, "The new 4.6-liter is taller than the previous 5.0-liter powerplant and requires a bit more space on the bottom. As a result, the chassis for the 1996 Mustang has been modified to permit numerous improvements." The new front cross-member provided additional strength and body rigidity. This allowed the engineers to revise the suspension geometry for less understeer, a common complaint about the first SN-95 cars. The GT also got a larger (24-mm) rear stabilizer bar and revised shock absorber tuning.

An AM/FM cassette became standard equipment; there were improvements to the passive anti-theft system; and the new 4.6 engine brought a larger exhaust system made of stainless steel instead of mild steel tubing. And how did those new pipes sound? Quite good actually. If the Mustang couldn't deliver the horsepower (at least in GT form) that the Camaro did, at least Ford knew that a deep, burbling sound is still an important element of a sport V-8-powered coupe; their pipe-benders did a fine job at preserving some pop and rumble in the exhaust note.

It's worth noting a few improvements on the V-6 side, as these cars represent more than half of Mustang sales. The base cars got the Thunderbird SC version of the 3.8-liter V-6—without the blower, of course—but that means a stronger block for smoother running. This tougher motor also meant a 5-horsepower increase to 150. Though most enthusiasts head directly for the V-8s, a V-6 five-speed Mustang is a surprisingly sporty car to drive. Though there is not nearly the aftermarket-parts availability for it that the 5.0 and 4.6 enjoy, it does respond to a few simple tweaks and bolt-ons, making for a less expensive (to buy and insure) machine that many enthusiasts would prefer to a similarly priced Honda or Toyota.

Though the performance ratings of the new 4.6-liter, overhead-camshaft V-8 were identical to that of the previous 5.0, most test numbers indicated a slight decrease in acceleration. The 4.6 GT was the subject of an *AutoWeek* AutoFILE test, wherein the magazine not only tests the car, but solicits input from owners. Their tests yielded a 0–60 time of 6.8 seconds against 6.5 for the last 5.0 they tested. But *AutoWeek* was quick to extol the virtues of new versus old, "But emphasizing drag-strip performance neglects some of the new engine's advantages . . . the GT's single-overhead cams are profiled to maximize mid-range torque, so there's no performance benefit in using the last 800 rpm or so. Yet the 4.6 is much smoother than the pushrod 5.0-liter V-8, from idle to the 6,000-rpm red-line. Any driver who minds the tach needle will find the 4.6 a more satisfying engine over the road. Survey respondents who have owned both 4.6- and 5.0-liter GTs prefer the overhead-cam engine almost unanimously."

Surprisingly, 1996 sales dropped compared to 1995 levels, from 185,986 to 135,620. A drop of 50,000 units in any year, especially one with so many enhancements, is disappointing. But by this time, the sport-utility vehicle and personal truck market was really coming into its own. Ford may have even taken a few of its own Mustang sales away with an all-new and stylistically trend-setting F-150 pickup truck, which debuted in January 1996 as a 1997 model. Trucks stealing sales from pony cars? Just about every industry analyst agreed that while the "specialty coupe" market has life, it has shrunk and that most of those sales were taken by trucks and sport-utility vehicles (SUVs). You only need look at the sales figures for both markets to see that it's true; either people's tastes and needs have really changed, or the truck/SUV boom is a fad. Some feel it's both.

The new-for-1996 grille caused some airflow problems—cars tended to run a bit on the warm side—so the grille was deleted for 1997 models. Other than that, 1997 was virtually a carryover year.

As of this book's printing, the car that was supposed to die at least once since 1979 is entering its 20th year.

The 1996 Mustang GT coupe and convertible. Other than the addition of a grille to the radiator intake-opening, which can barely be seen in this photo, the 4.6L Mustang looked virtually identical to the 1994–1995 cars from the front. *Ford Motor Company publicity photo*

A modern variation on the classic five-spoke theme, the new-for-1996 GT wheels were optional, in either this cut-and-polished finish or painted silver metallic. They are the same 17-inch size as the 1994–1995 optional GT wheels and carry 245-section, Z-rated tires. *Matt Stone*

The original Fox platform lived 15 years in the marketplace, and FOX-4 is now entering its fifth year. Fortunately, we've come a long way from Mustang II. Revisions for 1998 are modest and evolutionary, but the best one, at least for GT enthusiasts, is an increase of 10 horsepower—a return to the 225-horsepower rating that seemed to be such a magical combination from 1987–1992. The higher output was derived by revisions to the exhaust side of the 4.6-liter's single-overhead-cam head.

Other revisions were again fairly minor; the blister-shaped clock pod disappeared from the top of the dash and—hold on to your hat—the ashtray, cup-holders, and power receptacle layout in the console was revised. Ford also did a bit of value engineering: Air conditioning, power windows, power door locks, power deck-lid release, and a remote keyless entry system became standard equipment with no increase in price. More Mustang for less money.

But the best news may yet lie ahead.

Ford, like any manufacturer, makes it a public relations policy not to talk about a future product. But the Mustang and Ford magazine editors make it their business to snoop around and find out what's in store for Mustangs to come. One thing is for sure: There is a Mustang in Ford's future. The company admits to having a Mustang project engineering team in place and at work. If the platform were to continue untouched, there wouldn't be such a group on the payroll, so this alone is testimony to life in the old pony.

In mid-1997, both *SUPER FORD* and *Mustang Monthly* published articles that, in so many words, said the Mustang was off the mark and was not pleasing the real performance audience who was tired of

David Kimble, a world-renowned illustrator, produced this cutaway drawing of the new Mustang, highlighting the new engine and revised 17-inch wheel design. *Ford Motor Company publicity photo*

paying mid-$20,000 price tags for cars that could barely outrun a V-6 Camaro, much less the V-8. Each speculated on Mustang combinations that could or should be built, all of them centering around higher performance and lower cost. Clearly a certain portion of the buying public is happy with the cars, as Mustang regularly outsells Camaro and Firebird combined, horsepower or no. But it's also interesting to note that the V-6 is making up more and more of Mustang sales, now about 70 percent, as opposed to about 55 percent when the car was redone for 1994.

The answers to the magazines' questionnaires said the real performance buyer wants less costly cars with more performance and would be willing to accept lower equipment levels to achieve it. There was also a strong preference noted for a return to pushrod-engined cars, like the Cobra R. Ford reacted strongly to the magazines' charges. Fortunately the indication is that Ford is passionately committed to the Mustang, again having learned its lessons with watered-down versions in the past. But don't count on seeing pushrods again; the company—and fortunately SVO and SVT—are committed to smaller, more modern overhead-cam engines as the performance future for Ford, Mustangs, and otherwise.

As this book goes to press, magazines have recently carried spy photos of disguised mule cars wearing revised sheet metal for the 1999 model year. The changes include a deeper character line running down the side of the car, larger headlights, a square-jawed grille opening, and other changes to the front fascia. The intent is supposedly to make the Mustang look larger and more substantial.

With fans hoping for more horsepower, that too is both possible and probable. When Ford brought out the Romeo engine line, the virtues of the modular design and the overhead-cam engines' breathing capability were liberally extolled by Ford. Yet the best we've seen from the SOHC 4.6 is 225 horsepower. Rumor held that a 240- to 250-horsepower version was to appear for 1998, but it seems this will likely wait for the revised body. Other talk has had the pumped-up SOHC 5.4-liter V-8 coming out with outputs as high as 265 horsepower. It takes more than just pure horsepower to sell cars, but the true Mustang enthusiast would still appreciate something to show their F-car buddies. The revised 1998 F-car stays with overhead valves and gets a slightly detuned version of the new Corvette LS-1 V-8, which is rated at an impressive 305 horsepower and still backed by a six-speed manual transmission.

The Cobra may or may not be in for a horsepower injection of its own. We know that SVT's marketing and product arm has been begging Ford for a 5.4-liter version of the alloy, dual-overhead-camshaft engine, and supposedly at least one such engine has

The notable changes in the new Mustang—the removal of the clock from the top of the dash panel and the revised exhaust ports good for another 10 horsepower—can't be seen in Ford's official press photo of the 1998 model. But watch for new sheet metal in 1999. *Ford Motor Company publicity photo*

been on the test bed. Horsepower potential has been said to be an easy 350, but Ford also has to consider its own marketing face and the social responsibility of marketing such a model. Though the enthusiasts love it, the government and other regulatory types decree that any car with this much performance potential is dangerous and emblematic of a company not concerned with safety and the use of natural resources. Fortunately, we know better.

One thing that awaits—perhaps due for the 1999 or 2000 model year—is the long-anticipated independent rear suspension (IRS) system. Pontiac has said it has no intention of developing an IRS system for the Firebird, so we assume that goes for Chevrolet as well. One criticism of the Mustang, even in its most refined FOX-4 SVT Cobra form, is its tendency to get a bit tail-happy on bumpy roads, especially when those bumps show up during a hard-cornering maneuver. The IRS is said to be a slightly shrunken version of that used by the 1989–1997 Thunderbird and the Lincoln Mark VIII, which would be just fine as that system is effective in operation and reasonably cost effective to build. We hear the IRS for Mustang is a sure thing and should substantially increase its handling prowess.

New sheet metal. More horsepower. A new suspension system. Proof that the Mustang's original concept is still valid, and there is indeed life in the old pony yet.

A Mustang convertible comes down the line at Dearborn. Note that certain elements such as the glass, top, and brake system are in place; however, the engine and suspension have yet to be mated with the body and chassis. Automobile factories are certainly a better place to work than they used to be. You wouldn't have seen this much bright lighting, a special floor surface, and so many cooling fans in an automobile plant 30 or 40 years ago. This plant underwent a substantial retooling in preparation for the SN-95 Mustang. *Scott Mead*

# *six* SVE + SVT =

# Special Mustangs

Germany's BMW calls its cars "The Ultimate Driving Machines" and with good reasons. The company builds high-performance luxury coupes and sedans that many consider to be among the world's best automobiles. But within BMW there is a small division dedicated to building limited-production cars that are even more special than mainstream BMW models. The division calls itself M-Sport. American buyers know it through products like the M3 coupe and sedan and the M5 and M6 machines that preceded them. M-Sport's goal is simple: take the company's already supremely competent mainstream products and develop them to a higher level of performance, luxury, and exclusivity. Does it work? BMW sells every M model car it chooses to build.

A big day for SVT as 1993 Cobra Job 1 rolls off the line. John Plant, the founding manager of SVT, and Janine Bay, then in charge of SVE, see Job 1 off the line. *Special Vehicle Team*

*Matt Stone*

SVT's first Mustang endeavor was the 1993 Cobra. The front spoiler was a modified GT version, but the rocker-panel cladding gave up the GT's scoops in favor of a simpler look. The 17-inch wheels were the largest ever offered on a Mustang. The team that designed the 1994 Mustang speaks proudly about the reappearance of the "running horse" badge to the car's front grille area, but it actually appeared here first, one model year earlier, in the SVT Cobra's grille opening. *Special Vehicle Team*

Fortunately, BMW is not the only company that has the ability and foresight to invest the time, money, and effort into building limited-production specialty cars for what is surely a small percentage of the buying public. Ford, like BMW, Mercedes, and a few others, realizes the benefit from such an investment. There is a marketing advantage to having a discernible, high-performance line of cars and a halo effect on the rest of the company's products, not to mention the spirit that can be engendered within the company and the value in satiating the needs of its most ardent and enthusiastic customers. BMW has M; Ford has SVT.

SVT stands for Special Vehicle Team, and without sounding like a press release, the name fits. Its products are indeed special; the name of their game is vehicles, and the groups of people that develop and market the cars are indeed a team. Two teams really. SVT is the marketing, training, and customer relations arm, while Ford's Special Vehicle Engineering group

The limited-production 1993 Cobra R looks much the same as the 1993 SVT Cobra but can be distinguished by the different 17-inch wheels, which would show up as an option on the new-for-1994 Mustang GT, and by the lack of fog lights (not visible in this photo). However, on the Cobra R, the wheel centers were painted black with a polished rim, while they were finished in plain silver on the later production cars. *Matt Stone*

(SVE) is the entity that actually develops and builds the product. Though their functions are different, their purpose is the same (in their own words): "to use the best-available resources both from within and without Ford to explore new ways of creating and marketing high-performance vehicles for sale in limited numbers. This cross-functional team is charged with creating cars and trucks with distinctive personalities and high-performance capabilities . . . "

SVT and SVE were formed in late 1991 and officially announced in February 1992. The first products to be marketed under the SVT banner were set to debut as 1993 models—little more than a year after the formalization of both groups. A considerable task to be sure.

Ford had tried a similar experiment with the SVO just a decade before. It was less than a total success, having yielded just one model that was on the market for three years. SVO was never set up with adequate marketing support, dealer training, or public relations. But SVT's vision was larger and had "longer legs." They also learned some lessons from the previous experience. "Probably one of the biggest hurdles," according to Janine Bay, chief product engineer for Mustang, "was that previously we . . . had launched the SVO Mustang back in the mid-1980s and there was a lot of resistance because of that . . . however, the 1984–1986 SVO Mustang had not been supported in the marketplace with the sort of marketing effort that was to become one of the foundations of SVT." The fact that the SVO didn't perform as well as the much less expensive GT also certainly had something to do with it.

What drove the creation of SVT and SVE? "It was [Ford executives] Bob Rewey from the sales and marketing side and Neil Ressler from the product development side. They saw the vacancy . . . in the Ford product line-up, and they also saw the need to fill it," according to John Coletti, manager of Special Vehicle Engineering. "I was on Team Mustang at the time, but I distinctly remember the early meetings . . . were driven by those guys. And they are still very active [in SVT and SVE] today." Coletti was officially assigned to SVE in November 1991, and long-time Ford executive John Plant was put in charge of launching the SVT side of the equation. Curiously, and perhaps to SVT's benefit, Plant had also previously worked at BMW.

It would be one thing for any group to develop a specialty niche product in little more than a year's time, but SVT/SVE jumped into the fray with both feet, committing to two such vehicles for an early 1993 release: a Mustang, dubbed the SVT Cobra, and a dedicated high-performance shortbed pickup truck called the Lightning. Based on the popular F-150 shortbed and

A 235-horsepower version of the 5.0 was installed in the first 1993 SVT Cobras. The additional power was attributed to a revised intake system and cylinder heads, which were later offered through the SVO catalog and remain a popular after-purchase performance upgrade to non-Cobra cars. The engine's enhanced upper-end power could really be felt at 4,000 rpm and above, where the standard 205-horse 5.0 began to run out of steam. *Matt Stone*

powered by a special 240-horsepower, 351 Windsor V-8, the Lightning would set new performance and handling standards never before seen from a truck.

SVT knew that another "paint and tape stripe" special-edition Mustang would never do. If anything, the previous misuses of the Cobra name, such as the Mustang II King Cobra and the 119-horsepower Cobra Mustangs of the early 1980s had somewhat become mockeries. The Cobra had to have the hardware to deliver the goods in terms of performance, sophistication, and appearance. It's also worth noting Ford's commitment to the SVT concept by even allowing a 1993 Cobra to begin with. Keep in mind that tooling up for and certifying any vehicle is expensive, and even as SVE and SVT began developing the 1993 Cobra, the new SN-95 Mustang model was already well under way. It was a lot of work for what was already known to be a one-year-only model, but again this demonstrated that Ford was serious about the performance/niche market. Besides, launching the division with just the Lightning pickup would have given a completely inaccurate message about what SVT was all about. There was one final reason for pressing ahead with the single-year-only 1993 Cobra: General Motors was launching its first all-new Camaro and Firebird in a decade for 1993, and early reports

One of the world's best ways to ride off into the sunset would be in a 1996 SVT Cobra convertible. You can tell the 4.6-liter DOHC Cobras from the 5.0 models because of the additional bulges in the hood required to accommodate the intake system. *Matt Stone*

White-faced gauges have become an SVT trademark styling statement. Leather upholstery is an often-ordered option on all SVT Cobras, and the center of the steering wheel carries Cobra identification instead of Mustang. Other than that, the Cobra interiors are much the same as they are in a Mustang GT. *Matt Stone*

were that these cars would handily out-run and out-handle the standard Mustang GT. The special-edition, higher-performance Cobra model would give Ford and its SVT dealers something to sing about until the revised Mustang came along a year later.

There was no chance the first SVT Cobra would be criticized as a cosmetic job only, as it was hardware packed. Available only in hatchback form, the Cobra centered around the 235-horsepower 5.0 liter that represented the first major reconfiguration of the engine since 1987. The major changes that turned the 5.0 liter into a Cobra V-8 related to the engine's breathing, such as a new upper and lower intake manifold, revised heads with larger intake and exhaust ports, larger valves, and revised rocker arms sourced from Crane. The size of both the throttle body and mass air sensor were increased, and a different cam profile was specified. A higher-flow fuel pump and fuel injectors ensured more fuel to go with the increased airflow from the new intake tract, and the EEC-IV was re-calibrated to match.

Backing the new V-8 was a revised spec five-speed manual gearbox; no automatic would be offered. The

clutch was a higher-capacity unit; even the driveshaft was revised in preparation for the extra power. Enthusiasts had been crying for better brakes for years, and in that instance the Cobra really delivered. Gone were the rear drums, and in their places were vented rotors making the Cobra the first Mustang with four-wheel disc brakes since the SVOs in 1986. And with them came more rolling stock upgrades: huge finned alloy wheels finished in attractive metallic argent silver, sized 7.5x17.0 inches, wearing Goodyear 245/45 ZR17 speed-rated tires.

In keeping with SVT's philosophy of offering a balanced package, the Cobra received suspension upgrades to complement the increased horsepower, better brakes, and grippy tires. But SVT decided right up front that a race-car-like, buckboard ride was not what buyers wanted, and the Cobra was one of the first Ford products that attempted to calibrate the suspension components accordingly.

Lower, linear-rate rear springs were used in place of the GT's progressive-rate units as well as a smaller front stabilizer bar. However, the upper control arm bushings in the rear suspension were stiffer. Some of the compliance achieved by the softer springs was regained by the stiffer, lower aspect ratio tires and 17-inch wheels. The theory was called "controlled compliance," and SVT went so far as to have race drivers Bob Bondurant and Jackie Stewart evaluate the vehicles and provide feedback on the suspension tuning before the final specs were set. Short of going to an independent rear suspension, SVE was successful at taking what was a fairly old set of underpinnings and polishing up the ride and handling mix to levels not thought of when the first Fox Mustangs appeared nearly 15 years before.

All this go (and corning and stop) deserved a little show, so the SVT Cobra got a subtle but effective exterior redo. The front fascia was revised to include a grille element, and the GT's scooped lower valance panels were replaced with more conservative yet more substantial-looking cladding. New rear taillights were a new interpretation of those from the SVO, and a raised, square-shouldered wing sat atop the deck lid. Don't forget those Cobra badges. Only available in three colors (red, teal blue/green, and black), the SVT Cobra was a bold and mature interpretation of the Fox-bodied Mustang, some say the most attractive to come down the line.

The enthusiast press gushed over the SVT Cobra, the most common comments relating to the increased power, especially at the upper rpm ranges where the standard 205-horsepower 5.0 H.O. tended to taper off and the immensely improved braking performance. Also often praised was the improved grip that did not come at the expense of ride quality and the

The special assembly team poses with a 1995 Cobra R. Today's automobile plants are high-speed, highly automated facilities. The various components, color combinations, and options are programmed well in advance of the year's production cycle. To actually reprogram the line and the supplier body to build 250 cars to a special spec without hoods and many other normally installed components is a huge and costly undertaking. The efforts of SVO, SVE, SVT, the Dearborn assembly plant, Ford suppliers, and aftermarket shops combined to build one of the most interesting limited-edition production cars of recent memory. *Special Vehicle Team*

tasteful exterior package. Ford built 4,993 Cobras for 1993 on a goal of 5,000, so from that standpoint, it appears that SVT was accurate in gauging the demand and production capacity for this vehicle. Add to that 5,276 Lightnings, and SVT had built its first 10,000 vehicles in short order.

Launching a new division and two new models is one thing, but before the year was out SVT had yet another project in the works. Any Shelby Mustang was special, but even among them there were also *special* Shelby Mustangs. The street versions of those first rough-and-ready 1965 Shelby GT 350s were intended to homologate the model for the race track as much as anything. The real Shelby Mustang race car was called the "R-Model." Thirty-seven were built, most of them raced, and most of them won big time. They are among the most interesting and most collectible of Shelby models.

During the summer of 1993, not long before the new-for-1994 Mustang was to debut, Ford elected to let the Fox car ride out with one last blast and chose to use the "R" designation for a limited-production special race-intended model. Really an SVO-authorized project, the Mustang Cobra "R" Competition Package was targeted at improving Mustang's visibility and performance in both IMSA's Firestone Grand Sport Series and the SCCA's World Challenge Class B Series.

The Cobra R was an engaging "trip through the parts bins" at Ford as it received both special components intended for racing and was de-contented to save weight and cost. The suspension got a more-racer-like set of Koni shock absorbers, struts, uprated Eibach springs, and sway bars as the R's street-ride quality was not the issue. Engine cooling and brakes were upgraded as well, with the engine also getting an oil cooler. Axles were upgraded to five-bolt lug

Note the specially cast "5.8 Liter Cobra" badge atop the upper intake manifold on this 1995 Cobra R V-8. This engine was an interesting combination of marine, SVO, aftermarket, and R-specific componentry. *Special Vehicle Team*

A virtual "sea of Cobra R engines" awaits installation after the main cars were built at Dearborn. Many, but not all, of the 250-odd specially built 5.8s are in this historic photograph. *Special Vehicle Team*

patterns, and new 17-inch wheels with a polished rim and black center were specified. Recognize them? You should, as they appeared as an option on the SN-95 Mustang a year later.

Saving weight is of paramount importance in a racing application, so out went the air conditioning, fog lights, inner-fender panels, power windows, some sound deadening, and a myriad of other components that saved about 150 pounds over the weight of the SVT Cobra.

What made the first Cobra R so special was not its race history. It still didn't quite prove the match for the 275-horsepower Camaros on the race track. What makes it special is that SVO/SVT/SVE could even get the job done. Producing any sort of hand-built, limited-production, or special-edition product within a large industrial concern such as Ford is difficult, but the fact that the program was approved with the intent to build just 100 cars is little short of amazing. Actually, 107 competition Cobras rolled down the temporary assembly line. They were priced at $25,692, and all were spoken for before they were built. A special Mustang for sure.

# Hand Built for Speed
## SVT Mustang Cobra
## DOHC V-8

It's the oldest expression in cardom: "Whatcha got under the hood." You can talk paint, wheels, tires, wings, flares, and CD players until you're blue, but if the motor don't make it, the "Show Don't Go." Ford seems to have a world-beater on its hands with the new-for-1996, 305-horsepower SVT Mustang Cobra V-8. And the best news is that the surface of its potential has barely been scratched, though the aftermarket is already busy bolting on the blowers, nitrous, and other goodies. Over the next decade, it's likely to turn up in more than just Mustangs.

What makes this 4.6-liter, all-alloy, double-overhead-cam, four-valve-per-cylinder V-8 so special? Three words—design, hardware, and manufacture.

Through the 1970s and 1980s, American auto makers cruised along with engines that were products of the 1950s or 1960s, Ford included. While Mercedes, Infiniti, and Lexus had all come out with high-tech four-cam V-8s of their own by 1990, Ford and GM waited until 1993 to bring out theirs. It was worth the wait. Cadillac's 300-horsepower Northstar is a honker, and the Cobra motor is the crown jewel (so far) in Ford's "modular" engine family. The first version produced was a cast-iron, 4.6-liter, single-overhead-cam, 190-horse unit that came out in 1991. Next up, an aluminum DOHC version for the 1993 Lincoln Mark VIII rated at 280 horsepower; then finally the high-output Cobra version for 1996.

There are dozens of tech features that make all the engines in this design family a generation ahead of the old OHV domestic jobs. They employ metallurgical technology not even dreamed about in the flathead days. Connecting rods are "fractured," meaning the rod is cast as a piece, then literally snapped in two, creating an exact "break pattern" in the metal between the cap and rod. Each main cap and connecting rod will work only as a matched pair, but it also means they are a perfect fit. The engines have all been designed with fuel injection and computerized engine management in mind (rather than added on afterwards), so overall efficiency is improved. Another smart design feature is that most engine accessories, like the alternator, air conditioning compressor, and power steering pump are bolted directly to the block. No accessory brackets translates to less weight and greatly reduced vibration.

Besides all of the above, the Cobra powerplant goes several steps farther. Ford not only applied its own engineering expertise but the knowledge of other technology partners from around the world. It started with the alloy block, cast for Ford by Teksid of Italy. Their clients include other European manufacturers and even the Ferrari Formula I team. The crankshafts are forged, not cast, and run in six-bolt main bearing caps. The initial forging is done by Gerlach in Germany, with machining and final finish work performed at Ford's Windsor engine plant in Canada.

When increasing the size of the throttle body on an older Ford 5.0, a 70-mm, 77-mm, or 80-mm unit is considered a big move up. The Cobra mounts twin 57-mm units for a total of 114 mm of throttle body opening. There's also a set of electronically controlled port throttles, which act somewhat like the secondary tract on a four-barrel carburetor. They kick open at 3,250 rpm and make additional power right up to the 6,800-rpm redline. The intake system is aluminum as is the block and four-valve heads. The engine is about the size of an old Ford 351 Cleveland V-8, though several hundred pounds lighter, a bit lower, and somewhat wider due to the wide heads.

Perhaps the most interesting aspect of the engine is the way it is put together. Part of the allure of a pure racing engine is that it's carefully hand assembled with greater attention to balance and detail than the average motors that churn off an assembly line at 2,000 units per hour. Ford has essentially set up its own custom engine shop to build the SVT powerplants and calls it the Niche Line.

The Niche Line is a very special corner of Ford's Romeo, Michigan, engine assembly plant, where the balance of the modular engine family is built. Ford took an old truck dock, consulted with Krause of Germany and Thyssen Production Systems of Michigan, added a $3.4-million investment, and got a 10-station facility ready to build engines with a unique combination of hand assembly and computer- aided machinery. Emphasis goes on the hand-assembly part: Each station is manned—and this term is used loosely as the person who's in charge of the Niche Line is a woman named Lisa Cittadino—by two assemblers. They've been specially trained on the process and know every nut, bolt, and grommet in a 4.6 Cobra engine.

Working quickly and methodically, each two-person team can assemble a complete and running engine in a bit more than an hour. They are personally responsible for the job and have the authority to stop it cold if something isn't right. Every component is inspected prior to assembly. "They work closely with each other," commented John Clor, a member of SVT's public relations team who has followed engines through the Niche Line. "They alternate between selecting parts from bins, placing fasteners, operating the tools, inspecting the results, and checking off the process sheet." Lessons learned on the Niche Line have also made it back to mainstream production at Romeo as process improvements.

The final touch? The team places a special metallic "Mustang Cobra Engine" decal on the passenger-side cam cover of each unit . . . *then signs it*. Try to find the autographs of the guys who built the engine of your average Chevy or Honda.

If you are looking for a high-performance, internationally built, and hand-assembled engine, you shouldn't have to look farther than the 4.6-liter Cobra V-8. And the package it comes in (your choice of SVT Mustang Cobra coupe or convertible) ain't bad either.

*Specially trained team members hand-assemble Cobra's 305-horsepower, 4.6-liter alloy V-8. Note the use of gloves. Scott Mead*

SVT rightly considers the hand-assembled, 4.6-liter Cobra V-8 (center) to be among the best high-performance engines it has ever built. It is featured here with two other legendary blue-oval V-8s, the hemi-headed Boss 429 (left) and the 600-plus-horsepower 427 SOHC of 1960s drag-racing fame (right). *Special Vehicle Team*

A new Mustang for 1994 brought a new SVT Cobra as well—the 240-horsepower Cobra 5.0. Most of its driveline componentry was carried over virtually intact, though horsepower went from 235 to 240, but SVT judged that the new platform still had room for improvement. Even though the Mustang now had four-wheel disc brakes, SVT went an extra mile by installing huge 13-inch vented rotors up front and larger 11.65-inch rotors out back, again wanting to match the Cobra's braking ability with its increased horsepower rating over that of the GT.

The suspension system required a bit less modification than did the 1993 model, but in keeping with the "controlled compliance" philosophy, sway-bar sizes and spring rates were decreased just a bit. Another 17.0x8.0-inch wheel design appeared, and the exterior design package was also a bit less hardware-intensive than the last Cobra. The 1994 Cobra's front fascia replaced the GT's rectangular fog lamps with larger, round ones, and the air intake and front bumper were subtly reshaped. Nighttime visibility was improved via a "clear lens" headlamp design. A bit more curvaceously shaped spoiler adorned the rear deck lid. The rocker panels and side cladding were unchanged.

One feature that showed up in the first 1993 Cobra interior has since become a bit of an SVT trademark, that being white gauge faces. And for the first time, the Cobra would also be available in convertible form.

With Mustang being an all-new car, it goes without saying that 1994 was a big year. And to commemorate the occasion, Ford did the same thing it did the last time a new Mustang came to market: Pace the Indy 500. Red Cobra convertibles were chosen to pace the 1994 race, but this time a lot less work was required to get the Mustang up to pace car snuff. The engines for the three pace cars were largely stock 240-horsepower Cobra-spec 5.0s with a less-restrictive exhaust. Other modifications consisted of slightly revised spring rates (mostly to accommodate TV camera equipment), an on-board fire-safety system, a fuel cell to replace the standard gas tank, and the use of the automatic transmissions. Naturally there was the addition of required pace car lighting and a light bar, communications equipment, and special graphics.

Ford dug into a bit of both its own and the Indianapolis Motor Speedway's history with the selection of the three drivers that would drive the parade laps leading up to the start of the race. Alex Trotman, Ford chairman, would drive one car; four-time Indy winner A. J. Foyt would drive a second, and Indy winner and Trans-Am champ (in a Mustang) Parnelli Jones would drive the third. In addition, Jones would drive the actual pace laps before and during the race.

S VT Cobra's all-alloy 4.6 V-8 as installed in the 1996 Cobra. *Matt Stone*

The Cobras performed their pace car duties flawlessly during the race, though an all-Ford day was spoiled as a Mercedes-Benz-powered Penske driven by Al Unser Jr. won the race in rather convincing fashion. To commemorate Ford's participation in the event, SVT sold 1,000 special Pace Car Edition Cobras.

Having to deal with a one-year body style model for 1993 and an all-new platform for 1994 were arduous enough tasks, so things were relatively quiet for 1995—at least for SVT's street products. The 1995 Cobra carried over with little change, though the convertible, available only in black, became a standard model, having been offered only as a pace car version for 1994. But "The Three Ss" (SVO, SVE, and SVT) elected to develop a bit more speed-laced alphabet soup with another R model.

Mustang enthusiasts had been begging for more cubic inches, something to throw at their 350-cubic-inch-packing Camaro pals. Well unfortunately, they didn't get it in a pure street GT or Cobra model, but more

cubes did find their way into an all-new Cobra R model for 1995. Ford learned some lessons on the original Cobra R program of just a few years back: Demand easily exceeded 100 cars, and many of the cars were ending up in the hands of collectors and speculators, not racers. Changes to the 1995 R program would hopefully cure those issues. First, production was set for 250 units. Not only was there a $35,499 sticker price (plus a $2,100 gas-guzzler tax), but a more important credential was needed—a racing license.

Sound strange? Would this clandestine qualifier keep people away in droves? Not a chance; once SVT sorted through all the requests, license documentation, and orders, all 250 Rs were sold before they were built. Bring on those Chevrolets and Pontiacs in SCCA World Challenge and IMSA Grand Sport classes.

Actually, the beginning of the 1995 R program came just a few months after the 1994 Mustang's introduction when John Coletti and SVE were given the go-ahead to begin researching the concept of a new R based on the SN-95 platform. Two prototypes were built, and one was later driven by journalist Tony Swan in the Nelsen Ledges 24-hour enduro race. This seemed like an excellent opportunity to give the package a test. An accident kept the hand-built R prototype out of the winner's circle, but it was one of the fastest cars on the track. It was clear this competition Cobra would pack better performance than the original R.

T he SVT Lightning pickup was a companion to the Cobra in the SVT line-up from 1993–1995. Sales never met expectations, though it may have been just a bit ahead of its time as the performance pickup craze really began taking off just as the Lightning bowed out of the line-up. It also had the engine that many wanted in the Mustang GT or at least in the Mustang Cobra—a 5.8-liter Windsor V-8. *Special Vehicle Team*

Most of the changes to the 1997 Cobras could be seen in this photo, including the new green color and the option to order a Cobra without the rear trunk wing. *Matt Stone*

In addition to developing prototypes and engineering high-performance production models, one of SVE's charges, according to manager John Coletti, is to develop concept cars demonstrating the capabilities of SVE. In other words, they get to build hot rod toys using the best parts they can get their hands on. This particular project, based on a 1995 Cobra, packed a specially developed 6.1-liter (373-cubic-inch) Windsor V-8. Using a hand-built intake manifold and cold-air system, this bulge-hooded Mustang put out 350 horsepower. *Motor Trend* tested it, achieving a "tire frying" 5.2-second 0–60 time. The quarter-mile came up in just 13.3 seconds. No turbos, no nitrous, just cubic inches and crisp engine tuning got the job done. *Matt Stone*

The heart, literally and figuratively, of the 1995 Cobra R was a 351-cubic-inch (also called a 5.8-liter) Windsor V-8. Its architecture is much the same as the 302 with a longer stroke. As a matter of fact, this relationship is part of what made the engine swap feasible in the first place. Certifying an entirely new engine package for just 250 cars would have probably either killed the program or kept it to a 5.0-liter engine only. But Coletti, Steve Anderson, the R project's chief engineer, and company knew the car needed more, so they worked with the EPA and documented that the 351 Windsor was a close enough relative to the already-certified SVT 5.0; a less-stringent certification process was all that was required, and the R would have 351 cubic inches.

The engine was comprised of a Ford "marine" block with a custom camshaft, aluminum alloy pistons, forged steel connecting rods, SVO's "GT-40" heads and lower intake manifold, and a Cobra-specific cast-alloy upper intake. These special R engines were built at Ford's Windsor engine plant . . . in a day and a half. The Dearborn assembly plant and aftermarket vendors MascoTech and Jack Roush participated in a complicated assembly and testing process, not only for the engines, but for assembling the balance of the car.

The performance results from the specially brewed 5.8-liter Cobra R motor were outstanding: 300 horsepower at 4,800 rpm and perhaps and even more impressive, 365 lb-ft of torque at 3,750 rpm.

SVE's previous SN-95-based Mustang creation used a retro-tech Boss 429 "Shotgun" V-8 for power. But its newest toy, the Super Stallion, goes high-tech all the way, employing a hand built, supercharged, air-to-water intercooled 5.4-liter DOHC Cobra V-8 for power. In a politically correct nod to environmentalists, the 540-plus horse mod-motor will run on gasoline or E85 Ethyl alcohol fuels. This car began life as a 1995 Mustang Cobra but has been completely re-engineered by Coletti and his band of hot rodders; it was introduced at the Specialty Equipment Marketing Association show in November 1997. *MOTOR TREND* magazine tested the SS to a 0–60 time of 4.3 seconds, and it ripped off a standing quarter at 12.7 seconds at 112.8 miles per hour . . . on street tires, through the exhaust. Cost for this one off? Don't ask . . . *Matt Stone*

Some insiders say it was more. And it was emissions-certified and street-legal. Backing the husky 5.8 was a Tremec five-speed transmission; the standard Borg-Warner was deemed insufficient to handle the gaff of the bigger engine. A special 8.8-inch rear end with 3.27 gears was also fitted.

Like the previous R models, the 1995 R was intended for race track use. It was stripped of all unnecessary weight: air conditioning, power windows, some sound deadening, fog lamps . . . even the radio. You could get an R in any color you liked, so long as it was white with a beige cloth interior. As expected, the chassis was upgraded for improved handling (Eibach springs, Koni adjustable shocks, and firmer bushings). The intake manifolding was too tall for a standard hood, so a special fiberglass piece was sourced from the HO Fibertrends. Other racy bits included a 20-gallon Fuel-Safe fuel cell (fewer pit stops!) and accessory coolers for engine and power steering oil, and a special high-capacity, lightweight radiator was fitted.

Particularly significant were the special R-model wheels. At 17x9 inches, they were the largest wheels ever offered by the factory on a Mustang. They have since proved to be extremely popular in the aftermarket. A slightly smaller but similar design became the standard SVT Cobra wheel design for 1998.

The technical detail and specifications of the 1995 Cobra R go considerably beyond the scope of this book, but suffice it to say, it was a street-legal race

# Tim Boyd: SVT's Renaissance Man

## By Scott Mead

When Ford spun off its Special Vehicle Team (SVT) in 1991 as a brand name to showcase the talents of Ford's Special Vehicle Engineering (SVE) department, Ford pooled together a solid collection of automotive enthusiasts to transform mainstream products into something a bit more special.

Naturally, the person in the driver's seat of SVT had to be a gearhead, intimately in tune with what consumers wanted out of a limited-production car, and a proven team leader. John Plant got SVT off the ground beginning in 1991, but when it came time for Plant to move on to a well deserved retirement a few years later, Tim Boyd got the nod to fill the spot.

"I was probably picked for this job for two reasons," said Boyd. "Leading teams, because SVT is very much a team effort. I'm not the director so much. The team as a whole makes the decisions. Secondly, I'm known as a product guy, and you need product experience to do this job. This is an exciting job, but it's also a labor of love." It certainly didn't hurt that Boyd had been with Ford for most of his career, and was known as a car person within the ranks. Besides his love of 1960s-era muscle cars, Boyd is known as a world-class plastic-model kit builder.

According to Boyd, getting the performance job done is what the entire Special Vehicle Team is about. "Really, the purpose of SVT is to do two things: To develop a series of vehicles for our SVT dealers, which are profitable for them, and send a message to the enthusiast that Ford cares enough about this segment to develop the resources to build the kind of vehicles which appeal to these people. It's all about the four hallmarks of SVT: performance, substance, exclusivity, and value. The Cobra is more than just a go-fast pony car. This is, by far, the best value equation in the marketplace. For under $30,000, it's a very prestigious car which holds its resale value well.

"SVT works at Ford because there are so many people here who love great cars and trucks, but they don't necessarily have jobs which directly relate to that. But when you go to Dearborn Assembly, or Romeo, SVT works well there because there are enthusiasts right on that assembly line and in the office up front. Those are the people who are anxious to spend the extra time it takes to do a project like this. They want to be associated with these low-volume niche cars."

The mission of Tim Boyd and the future of SVT can only be described as an enthusiast's dream: "We want to continue to produce a series of limited-edition vehicles targeted for the serious driving enthusiast—those who want more than a big engine, but want larger brakes, a sophisticated chassis tuned to get compliant handling and ride quality, and the interior and exterior refinements which go along with it. The Cobra is and will continue to be our flagship, and we will continue to enhance it in the future. As for myself, I want to see SVT continue to develop and evolve and have ever more confident and exciting products. For the long term, we will see more fun stuff from SVT."

SVT's current chief, Tim Boyd. Matt Stone

car in every sense of the word. Every fourth Mustang built between February 28 and March 2, 1995, was destined to be a Cobra R. This was only a little more than a year after the go-ahead was given to build the prototypes. Besides a fast car, a successful race car (see chapter 9), and a highly collectible Mustang, the 1995 Cobra R is another example of what can happen when a group of enthusiasts within a large company conspire with management, the assembly workers, and the aftermarket to build something special.

In its first three years in the marketplace, SVT and SVE built and marketed a high-performance pickup truck, two different versions of the Mustang Cobra, plus two race cars and an Indy 500 pace car. Time to relax and enjoy the spoils? Not a chance, as SVT had new engines to deal with.

Because the days of overhead-valve-engined Mustangs were over, a new powerplant was being readied for the Cobra. And SVT finally delivered the engine Mustang enthusiasts had been begging for since the first 280-horsepower Romeo DOHC V-8 appeared in the Lincoln Mark VIII for 1993. Rated at 305 horsepower, the new SVT Cobra V-8 was something special (see sidebar). It was hand-built on a special production line and possessed specifications equaling that of many high-priced European exotic cars. Perhaps just as importantly from a marketing and exclusivity standpoint, the all-alloy "mod motor" was developed for and would only be used in the SVT Cobra. So this special Mustang now had a special powerplant that was all its own.

Other changes for 1996 were relatively minor. With the engine came even larger, 3-inch tailpipe ends (more for the sound than any performance advantage) and slightly firmer suspension calibrations. The earliest 4.6 Cobras tended to run a bit warm, and SVT initiated a quick fix in the form of substantial upgrades to the cooling system. The rear wing was now a customer-delete option, and the 4.6's higher deck height necessitated a revised hood with twin power-bulges to make room for the intake system.

One appearance option that drew comment, although not always praise, was the addition of "Mystic Clearcoat" paint. Mystic is a special set of colors developed by GAF, first available in a production car application on the 1996 SVT Cobra. Depending upon the light conditions at the time and exactly where you were standing, Mystic looked either green, purple, blue, black, or combinations of any or all of those. It was one of those "gotta have it" or "wouldn't dream of it" type of things, but it was distinctive nonetheless. It was offered on the Cobra coupe for 1996 only, at a cost of $815.

And just how did the new Cobra perform? Its numbers made it one of the best-performing Mustangs of all time, handily outrunning some of the 1960s models that many feel were the "real" performance Mustangs. *Road & Track* once again staged their Ford versus Chevy runoff, this time pairing a new four-valve, 4.6-liter SVT Cobra against a formidable and specially built Camaro SS. A ram-air system gave the Chevy a boost from 285 horsepower to 305 . . . a dead-on match for the Cobra's power rating.

The results were closer than they had been in years:

|  | 0-30 | 0-60 | 0-100 | 1/4 mile |
|---|---|---|---|---|
| SVT Cobra | 2.2 | 5.9 | 15.1 | 14.4 |
| Camaro SS | 2.1 | 5.9 | NA | 14.4 |

*all in seconds

Even the prices were almost a dead heat: $26,505 for the SLP (Street Legal Performance) built Chevy and $26,745 for the SVT Cobra. *R & T* gave the Camaro the slightest edge in the handling department but liked the Mustang better in terms of comfort, visibility, entry/exit, and just ease of driving. In the end, the Mustang was the car of choice, but no two cars could have made for a more interesting contest.

In 1996 the SVT Cobra had a banner year as the market responded to the high-horsepower engine offering. While SVT was on target with just over 5,200 Cobras sold for 1995, a total of 10,006 SVT Cobras were sold for 1996. It's also worth noting that this figure was achieved without the Lightning in the line-up, which bowed out at the end of 1995.

When the 1997 Cobra came off the line, a new paint color, Pacific Green Clearcoat, was introduced, and the rear spoiler became a customer-delete option. The honeycomb front grille, which only appeared the year before, was deleted. The grille was thought to contribute to overheating.

There was a rumor that a 5.4-liter version of the SVT Cobra V-8 would appear for 1998, but it didn't happen; perhaps a new mill will surface with the Mustang's revised bodywork for the 1999 model year. Still, there were a few changes that kept the 1998 SVT Cobra fresh, including two new colors (bright yellow and medium blue metallic) as well as a new 17-inch, five-spoke alloy wheel design that emulates the wheels used on the 1995 Cobra R.

Unlike the worthy but short-lived SVO project, SVT has demonstrated Ford's commitment to the concept of maximizing its mainstream products with specially built performance versions. The SVT/SVE teaming appears here to stay and will continue to develop niche products for small but demanding portions of the market. Hopefully, at least one of those products will always be a Mustang.

According to sources at Ford, 1998 is supposed to be the final year of the current Mustang body style. A freshened SN-95-based look is scheduled for 1999. This is a 1998 Cobra, replete with its first new wheel treatment since 1994, a style quite similar to that of the 1995 Cobra R. *Special Vehicle Team*

RIGHT ABOVE

Hokey PR photo though it may be, this shot accurately outlines the SVT Cobra's participation as the pace car for the 1994 Indianapolis 500. From left, former Indy 500 winner and lead pace car driver Parnelli Jones, Ford Chairman Alex Trotman, and USAC all-time win leader A. J. Foyt. With all due respect, Mr. Trotman, you don't need to point at Turn 1 for these guys; with five Indy 500 wins between them, they know how to get there. *Special Vehicle Team*

RIGHT

SVT has not marketed a Cobra R since 1995, but this specially built Bob Bondurant "school car" would certainly pass for one. The first 10 SVT Cobras were modified by Roush Technologies for use by Bondurant beginning in mid-1987 with the intent to ultimately replace the entire "pushrod fleet" with them by the year 2000. Roush developed a straightforward round of modifications that produced fast, safe, and predictable cars. *Matt Stone*

# *seven* The Saleen

# Connection

Call Saleen Performance anything you like, but don't call them a "tuner." It is a small-volume manufacturer in every sense of the word. For more than a dozen years, Steve Saleen and his cadre of engineers, assemblers, fabricators, and hot rodders have been turning garden-variety Mustangs into Saleen Mustangs. And a Saleen Mustang is something altogether different than just another "tuner car." The net result may appear somewhat the same: a Mustang that's received an array of performance, handling, and appearance upgrades. Many small Mustang shops claim to build "limited edition" Mustangs. This may be true, but more often than not, they've been limited to a handful of cars. Saleen has built more than 4,000. So, there's a difference.

The difference comes down to Steve Saleen himself. Saleen's enthusiasm for Mustang's began like most people's: "I was, at an early age, bitten by the racing and Mustang-heritage bug . . . I was very Ford-oriented in the late 1960s and early '70s. I had a '65 Shelby, a '66 Shelby, and my dad had a '66 289 coupe. I also had a '67 GT fastback that looked like Steve McQueen's car in [the movie] *Bullit*, except that [McQueen's car] had a 390 in it, and I put dual quads on it. I then went on to a '69 Boss 302." Saleen admits to being a "Ford guy" through and through; transforming Camaros, Hondas, or something else into limited-production, high-performance specials was never in the cards.

Saleen was also an avid racer with considerable talent. He began racing a Porsche originally owned by his father, then progressed to SCCA Formula Atlantic competition. In 1980 he finished third in that series championship; the competition must have been formidable as Jacques Villenueve won the title. He began competing in SCCA Trans-Am in 1982, the year Ford came out with the revised Mustang 5.0-liter HO GT. Saleen formed his own company—originally called Saleen Autosport—in 1984,

*E. John Thawley III*

The Saleen Performance facility in Irvine, California, is home to the production plant, customer service and repair shop, parts and accessory showroom, offices, and the parts warehouse. The Speedlab race cars are built and maintained in a different facility. Four 1997 Saleen Mustangs await delivery to Ford dealers; you cannot purchase one direct from Saleen. *Matt Stone*

A Saleen Mustang can begin life as either a Mustang GT, V-6, or SVT Cobra. The 351-powered cars start out as V-6s. Because the engine and the balance of the drivetrain all are removed, it makes no difference how the cars were originally equipped. Approximately 10 cars are working their way through the assembly/conversion process at any given time. *Matt Stone*

with the idea of building special Mustangs, while casting an eye to the racetrack.

From his experience owning several Shelby Mustangs, it was not lost upon the business school graduate that something resembling the Shelby phenomenon could happen again. He saw an opportunity with the late-model 5.0-liter Mustang. "As I progressed through my racing career, I saw an opportunity, with Ford and the Mustang, to do something similar to what, during my teenage years, I fell in love with." He set up shop in Long Beach, California, and the first three Saleen Mustangs were built off of 175-horsepower, 1984 models.

From the beginning, Saleen's goal was to improve the car from all aspects; a show-only looker would never do, and a fast car with no improvements to the handling would also be an imbalance. Saleen and buddy Paul Pfanner conceived and designed a comprehensive appearance upgrade package, including rocker panels, a rear spoiler ("Porsches have wings, Saleens have spoilers," according to Steve), and a square-shouldered front air dam. He dubbed his suspension improvement system "Racecraft," the name still used today for all Saleen suspension componentry. The package included Bilstein gas shocks and struts, special springs, urethane sway-bar bushings, and an additional chassis cross-member for added rigidity. Hayashi racing wheels were mounted with Goodyear Eagle GT tires.

Being a marketing major, Saleen knew the value of brand identity, so there was a plethora of Saleen identification on the car: specially screened gauges, badges on the dash, a Saleen Mustang decal at the top of the windshield, even Saleen ID on the chromed air-cleaner cover. And again taking a note from the Shelby legend, Steve knew it was important that the cars be numbered in such a way as to commemorate their place in what he hoped would be a long production history. Curiously, the first three cars were numbered 32, 51, and 52. Smart—many a producer was sunk by the media for showing prototype # 001.

In a marketing move similar to the old Hertz/Shelby program, Saleen S-281s are now available at Budget Rent-A-Car. The rental Saleens are virtually identical to the standard cars, and the convertibles have proved quite popular in rental fleet use. *Saleen Performance*

Saleen then hit the marketing trail, both with Ford and with the media. In short, the magazines loved the new Saleen Mustang. Performance-hungry enthusiasts were still recovering from the pre-1982 doldrums, and Steve's car easily out-handled the TRX-equipped factory Mustangs. It was too early in the development stage for any horsepower add-ons, but those would come in time.

A crucial turning point in the future of Saleen Autosport was gaining factory recognition from Ford. With that Saleen gained the ability to buy factory-direct new Mustangs and sell his cars through Ford dealers. This separated Saleen Mustangs from other "tuner cars." For 1985 Saleen had secured both.

The 1985 Saleens had more content than the earlier cars, and large-scale conversion began with these models. There were more interior upgrades, a 170-mile-per-hour speedometer and leather trim for the steering wheel and shifter. More exterior trim was added to differentiate a Saleen from a regular Mustang. But more important was further suspension development. The latest 225/60 Goodyear Gatorback tires were used. Again there were no modifications to the engine, though recall that 1985 was the year horsepower went from 175 to 210 anyway, so that increase was deemed enough . . . for now. Production increased from 3 to 128 cars, and Saleen appeared to be on his way.

Further developments and a return to the race track were noted in 1986. Saleen switched to Koni shocks and 16-inch Hayashi wheels and began installing a strut-tower brace. Steve has always been heavily involved in the design and specifications for the cars, and the Saleen Autosport urethane body-panel packages were constantly being updated for a smoother look and higher quality. The 1986s also had special racing-style front seats, upgraded stereos, and a Hurst shifter. Saleen knew the more content he could engineer into the car, the better. Ford's dealers received special training regarding how to best tailor the car to meet the desires of the owners and had specific ordering procedures. Though the first cars were white with blue trim, Saleen Mustangs could now be ordered in a variety of colors and in either the hatchback or convertible body styles. During the 1986 model year, 199 cars rolled out of Saleen's shop.

Saleen always kept one eye on his growing car business and the other on the race track. He believed his cars were ideally suited to SCCA's Showroom Stock Endurance class and entered a team of Saleen Mustangs in the series. Their first win came on a rainy day in the 24-hour enduro at Mosport. It would be the first of many.

Ford redesigned the Mustang for 1987, and so the Saleen was updated as well. The exterior aerodynamics package was completely redesigned with considerable attention being paid to the rear wing and lower rear-valance area. The brake system really got some attention in the form of five-lug SVO hubs, front and rear ventilated rotors, a heavy-duty master cylinder, and braided brake lines. It was expensive and labor intensive, but worth it, given the base car's marginal brake package. The interior upgrades were redesigned around Ford's revised cabin. With horsepower up to an all-time high of 225, the Saleen Mustang represented a performance bargain at $19,900. Saleen sales again increased to 278, including the five SCCA race cars.

Saleen re-entered the SCCA SS Endurance Series for 1987 and came out with guns blazing. An all-female win, with Desiré Wilson and Lisa Cacares sharing the driver's seat, notched the team's first victory of the season

A Vortech supercharged S-351 engine begins with the basic engine found in the SVT Lightning truck, though the entire top end is different. The Saleen intake, cam, heads, supercharger, and other modifications double the horsepower from 240 to approximately 500, according to Saleen. Note the Saleen ID plate in the upper right corner of the firewall. *E. John Thawley III*

A big day for fans of American muscle as two Saleen Mustangs (interestingly dubbed "Saleen Fords" on their pit signage) make their debut at Le Mans in 1997. Though neither car finished, they were extremely well received in Europe and were ultimately sold to buyers there after the 1997 race. Le Mans does pomp and circumstance like few other race events; each car is draped with a flag representing the team's home country, and the flags are removed just prior to the start of the race. *Saleen Performance*

at Sears Point. Wins followed at Portland and again at Mosport with a stunning first-, second-, third-, fourth-, and sixth-place performance for the three-car and *two-truck* team at Atlanta, running in two different classes. Saleen began to attract the attention and participation of a few of the more seasoned, but certainly most capable, drivers: former Trans-Am champs George Follmer and Parnelli Jones, to name just two. The team's effort was rewarded with the 1987 SCCA SS Endurance Series championships for team, manufacturer, drivers, and tires.

After many changes in 1987—in concert with the redmodel that the Mustang got from Ford—1988 was largely a carryover year for Saleen. But there were a lot of detail refinements. There was a switch to Monroe shock absorbers, and somewhere along the way Saleen began swapping the factory mufflers for Walker units. Sales continued to increase, and more dealers were added to the Saleen network. Remember the cars could

The expression "big kid's candy store" has probably been worn out, but it absolutely fits the Saleen Performance showroom. Here an SN-95 chassis is displayed on a dolly, making it easier to understand the purpose and placement of many of Saleen's chassis- and handling-upgrade components. *Matt Stone*

be financed through Ford and were fully warranteed by both Ford and Saleen. Though the race team could not back up 1987's championship performance, 1988 was the year for one particularly sweet victory, that being a 1-2-3 finish at Mosport. This Canadian venue was the site of the team's first win in 1986, and the 1988 win was its third consecutive victory at this track.

A fair assessment of 1989 could be—the best of times and the worst of times for Saleen. Though the Saleen Mustangs had been universally praised for their handling performance, improved interiors, and aggressive styling, people were crying for more horsepower. As the content level grew, the cost of a Saleen Mustang had escalated farther and farther above that of the LX and GT models. Buyers were asking for more horsepower as part of the bargain. They got it, and a bit more, in the form of the 1989 Saleen SSC.

Nobody wanted to increase performance in his cars more than Steve Saleen and his people did. But it wasn't that easy. By this time there was lots of go-fast hardware already on the market for the fuel-injected 5.0, but not a lot of it was EPA legal. In order to deliver the type of product he wanted and to be able to sell it as a new car through Ford dealers, the cars had to be smog legal and not void Ford's warranty parameters at the same time. This made the job a little tougher than just sliding in a cam, bolting on some headers, and delivering them to dealers' lots. Besides, emissions-certifying an engine is not an inexpensive proposition.

Saleen used car 87-01 (meaning car #01 of the 1987 model year; all Saleens are so numbered) as the development platform for the faster Saleen that would become the SSC. In typical hot-rodder fashion, the improvements were found by increasing the engine's breathing capability. The final package ended up with an enlarged throttle body, an AirSensors TPI unit, polished and ported heads, revised rocker-arm ratios, and stainless-steel headers replacing the factory units. They were backed up by Walker Dynomax mufflers. For even a bit more grunt, a 3.55 rear-end ratio was dropped in.

The SSC also got a revised graphics package, new five-spoke 16-inch wheels and even more chassis stiffening via a roll bar and rear chassis support, in addition to all the normal Saleen suspension and braking upgrades. Saleen bolted on the best hardware he could muster, everything from Monroe driver-adjustable shocks to special Saleen/Flowfit leather seats and a Kenwood CD player. CD players in cars were still a bit of a novelty at the time. Horsepower was estimated at 292, and this stormer would easily top 150 miles per hour. All of the 160 SSC fastbacks were sold in a heartbeat for their $36,500 asking price. Why didn't Ford jump on this package and create a real 25th Anniversary Mustang once it became clear that the Roush twin-turbo car would never see the production light of day? Good question because sales of the 1989 Saleen Mustangs were again the best in the company's history.

Saleen's racing efforts went big time for 1989, but it was an unfortunately short trip and a rough one at that. Saleen, like any American-born and bred race driver, wanted to race in the Indianapolis 500. Fortunately, his visibility, sponsor support, and a certain level of success in the car business allowed him to assemble an IndyCar team. Though it was a competent effort, it was small when compared to the manpower and budgets displayed by teams like Newman-Haas and Penske. Saleen's month of May was riddled by crashes and blown engines. The team did not qualify for the race, and Saleen had little more than a flattened checkbook to show for a valiant effort.

One of the keen advantages of being a small-volume producer such as Saleen is the ability to quickly redevelop the products and introduce special models as desired. This focus describes the model line-up from 1990 through the end of the Fox cars in 1993. For 1990, Saleen continued to offer Mustangs powered by the standard 5.0 liter, an uprated version first developed for the SSC. Now called the SC, the hot version quickly became popular as enthusiasts got the power to match the handling, equipment levels, and looks they were buying with the rest of the Saleen package. Throughout these model years, there were continuous upgrades

Steve Saleen and actor/comedian/driver Tim Allen pictured in front of Saleen/Allen Speedlab RRR team transporter and 1995 team car. The horse graphic on the trailer is repeated on the side of the car. Saleen says Allen "jokes constantly in the pits and over the radio, but when he straps on that helmet, he is all business." *Saleen Performance*

and changes to the aero package, wheels and tires, and interior trim. Some of the more notable improvements included: the 1991 cars got a 70-mm mass airflow sensor to replace the 65-mm unit; a 77-mm unit came just a year later; the first "Spyder" package arrived in 1992 with a hard tonneau covering up the convertible top and rear seats—giving the look of a two-seat roadster; the same year, a Vortech supercharged engine became optional; and 17-inch wheels were added. Saleen, his longtime production chief Jimmy Moore, Liz Saleen, and the entire crew were constantly busy developing new products for the cars and to support the thriving aftermarket parts business that grew out of it.

Saleen's 10th year in the business was 1993. His company built 10 black-and-gold 10th Anniversary edition cars to commemorate the occasion. Saleen's Mustangs kept getting better, further distancing themselves from the mainstream Mustangs. The only problem was business. In terms of sales and structure, it got worse.

"From the tail end of 1989 to 1993, I would call those our 'dark years,' " Saleen said. "That was not a very

The 1988 SCCA Endurance victory at Mosport: a 1-2-3 finish and the third Saleen win in three years at this venue. *Saleen Performance*

Saleen's personal 1995 SR-351 has yellow accents to match the exterior and special lightweight racing seats. The rear wing closely resembles that of the Saleen/Allen race car. Note the ancillary double-gauge pod atop the dash replacing the standard clock. *Matt Stone*

happy time in our endeavor. Nineteen ninety-two was probably our darkest year in that we only produced 17 cars . . . however, I think the key figure is that we actually produced 17 cars! About half-way through 1989 [the same time as the Indy qualifying effort], the economy went into a significant recession. The automobile industry was not excluded from that and was also hard hit . . . a lot of [large and small] companies went out of business.

"The company was fairly leveraged at that time in terms of capitalization, and as our [sales] volume shrunk, it was difficult to keep our doors open. What I did in trying to preserve the company was to take two alternatives. One was to [sell] our parts division lock, stock, and barrel to a couple friends. I took the car company portion . . . and settled on one particular group of investors that came in and basically said that if I would sign over the assets and the company to them, they would then put in money and take the company public, [so] they would be able to pay off the debts, [so we could all] move on with our lives. I took that option . . . and after I got into it a lot deeper, I found that the individuals I got hooked up with had misrepresented [their capabilities] and really had

no intention of doing what they had said they would. I found myself between a rock and a hard spot."

It took years for Saleen to work out the financial recapture of the company and, in fact, his own name as it applies to Mustangs. He did prevail, but the company was in shambles. Saleen freely admits that some employees lost their jobs, and many vendors had to wait for their money, but he worked diligently to support the customer base they had tried so hard to develop. In 1993 he formed a new company, Saleen Performance. He built a new shop in Irvine, California, and started almost from scratch.

The SN-95 Mustang could not have come along at a better time, and in 1994 things began a swift turnaround for Saleen. "I started calling on dealers to rebuild our network, took a partner named Tony Johnson who could bring some financial backing and astute business knowledge . . . and concentrated on building cars again."

Saleen designed an all new car based on the new-for-1994 Mustang, and it centered around what Mustangers had wanted for ages: a 351 Windsor V-8. The Saleen S-351 capitalized upon all that was good about the SN-95

Mustang, and then delivered what Ford didn't. A new aero package cured the Mustang's somewhat clumsy "bladed" rocker-panel treatment, and the front and rear treatments were the most aggressive yet. The new car's generous fender-well room allowed optional 18-inch Saleen Speedline magnesium wheels with the latest 35-series Z-rated rubber. Naturally the Racecraft suspension was recalibrated for the new car. The S-351 could be ordered in coupe, convertible, or speedster form.

But the heart of the S-351 lay beneath the composite hood: a 351-cubic-inch Windsor "crate motor" that Saleen converted to roller tappet form. Aluminum Edelbrock heads were fitted along with a heavily reworked SVO GT40 upper and lower intake. Developing this engine meant a lot of research and development work:

The cam was custom ground, the ignition recurved, and ceramic-coated headers with a new Borla exhaust system were added. AER, which also provides engine-building services to SVO helped with engine assembly. The Saleen-tweaked engine reportedly offered 370 horsepower at 5,100 rpm, and 422 lb-ft of torque at 3,500. Some suggest the horsepower figure may have been a little bit optimistic, but it's clear the S-351 was something completely different than your everyday 5.0.

For instance, 0–60 times were in the low-to-upper fives depending upon who was doing the testing. Perhaps more impressive was the handling performance. *Road & Track* tested an early S-351 and recorded a 0.97 g on the skid pad, as good or better than many models from Porsche or Ferrari.

The resemblance between the 1985 Saleen Mustangs for street and track was no accident. Saleen hoped that previous and current successes as a racer would help sell street cars. It certainly worked for Shelby, and once official recognition came from Ford Motor Company, it worked for Saleen as well. *Saleen Performance*

The first Saleen that improved on the factory muscle under the hood, the Saleen SSC, was also an exceptionally good handling car for the time. Saleen had moved away from the basket-weave-style Hyashi wheels to a more modern five-spoke design, and the graphics on the SSC were quite simple. A genuine SSC is quite collectible today as well as still being a hoot to drive. *Saleen Performance*

Another spark that ignited the turnaround for Saleen was the opportunity to get hooked up with actor/comedian Tim Allen. Saleen offered Allen, quite a car buff, some time behind the wheel, and Allen was quickly hooked. He asked Saleen to build him a special Mustang, and that was the birth of a pearl-white 1993 fastback dubbed "R-R-R." Sound familiar? It was named after the grunting noises of Allen's *Home Improvement* character, Tim "the tool man" Taylor.

That particular car is a one-off, Vortech-supercharged 302-powered Saleen Mustang—perhaps better suited to the track than the street. It also has a hand-fabricated front-end section using slimmer Ford Thunderbird headlights, several custom carbon-fiber panels such as the hood and front fenders, and aerodynamic wheel discs somewhat reminiscent of those used by IndyCars at the time. There are custom touches everywhere: racing pedals, a high-tech sound system, and a roll cage—the budget and the imagi-

nation were just about unlimited in the creation of what may be the ultimate Fox-bodied Saleen Mustang. Said to be good for 575 horsepower twisting through the Tremec five-speed transmission, the car has been clocked to a traction-limited 0–60 time of 4.9 seconds.

It was during an R-R-R test session at Willow Springs Raceway that Steve Saleen began to notice Allen's natural driving talent. "I would tell him to put the car 'over here' on the next lap [referring to an apex or cornering point], and he would hit it perfectly," Saleen said. "He listened, and learned, quickly." It wasn't long before the two formed the Saleen/Allen Speedlab RRR race team, the goal being SCCA's World Challenge class. World Challenge cars somewhat resemble what a modern Trans-Am car might look like if they were built from production Mustangs and had to retain certain stock body parts and chassis layout and suspension design elements. They typically compete

Just say "R-R-R" like Tim Allen does. Allen's "cost no object" special may serve as the ultimate expression of the Fox-bodied Saleen Mustang. Wheel covers were inspired by Penske Indy racers of the day, and the entire front end was custom-molded for this car. *Saleen Performance*

SN-95-bodied Saleen S-351. Even in naturally aspirated form, the S-351 gave Mustang owners what they wanted: the cubic inches that Ford never did. Painting the taillight bezels didn't help as much as the new taillight design that came in 1996. *Saleen Performance*

Like the nickname for Boeing 747 jets, Saleen calls its SR a "widebody." The bodywork is obviously inspired by the Saleen/Allen World Challenge race car. It is several inches wider at the rear hips and at the front fenders. This car, the first built, uses a BASF "Extreme" paint scheme similar to the Mystic paint option first seen on the 1996 Mustang Cobra coupe. The rear wing is as bodacious as they come, but then again, nothing about the SR is weak-spirited. Power comes from the blown 351 V-8. *Randy Lorentzen photo, courtesy Saleen*

against Porsches, Lotuses, Corvettes, Camaros, and other Mustangs.

Allen progressed quickly as a driver, and the team hit the trail for the 1995 season. Several guest drivers also participated depending upon need and schedule, including Price Cobb and Cobra-meister Bob Bondurant. There were victories that season, but the effort really paid off the following year when the sophomore-season team won the SCCA World Challenge Manufacturer Championship. This, added to the Mustang championship in 1987 and a subsequent SCCA Racetruck championship in Ford Rangers, puts three SCCA titles on Saleen's resume.

Hot on the heels of the S-351 came a supercharged version. The Vortech-blown Saleen S-351-R is rated at around 500 horsepower, fully smog and OBD II legal and warranteed by Saleen. AER participated in the development and does some of the assembly. All this horsepower costs money, so beginning in 1996 Saleen developed a more cost-effective car—the S-281—based on the new 4.6-liter Mustangs. The 281 moniker refers to the engine's cubic-inch rating. The S-281 still features all the suspension, interior, and exterior upgrades as the blown 351 cars but at a much more affordable price: $29,500 for an S-281 coupe as opposed to $53,900 for the S-351-R.

As the old saying goes, "Speed costs money. How fast do you want to go?"

Most S-281s are based on the two-valve, 4.6-liter cars, though some have been built using the 305-horsepower SVT Cobra as a base. What an unusual combination: a car that is a limited-production SVT Mustang with a hand-assembled engine *and* a numbered, limited-edition Saleen at the same time.

Saleen's marketing intelligence is displayed in the way his company courts dealers and customers and constantly reinforces the company's position as a Department of Transportation-recognized manufacturer. The Saleen showrooms conspicuously display aftermarket parts, accessories, and clothing. There is the Team Saleen club, a web site, a newsletter, and club open-houses at the factory. Steve Saleen makes many guest appearances, an effort to stay in touch with his customers. In business school, they call it "relationship marketing," and Saleen does it well.

What's next? You need only look at the unusually colored Saleen SR prototype pictured herein. With both a widened body and an independent rear suspension developed in concert with the racing effort, this may be the ultimate Saleen Mustang. Mustang enthusiasts love the fact that he continues to build cars that stretch beyond the mainstream.

# *eight* Mustangs and the

# Aftermarket

It's been said that "the aftermarket taught the Mustang how to drive." That may be a bit of an overstatement as it has always "driven" and, in many instances, driven quite well. But the aftermarket has enabled Mustangs to drive faster, handle better, stop shorter, and in some cases look better (at least more individualized than they did when they rolled out of Dearborn).

The Mustang has also been called "the '55–'57 Chevy of the '80s and '90s." Ford fans should take that as a compliment, because the '55–'57 Chevrolets are classics, noted as being inherently good and worthy designs. They became the building blocks for many memorable late-model hot rods and drag racing and show cars. Those Chevys were inexpensive, reasonably light, and responded exceptionally well to both minor and major performance tuning.

The same can be said of the Fox and FOX-4 Mustangs. The basics were there—particularly in 5.0 LX form—a V-8 engine and hearty driveline in a nicely sized package available at a reasonable price. Yet part of the appeal is that the Mustang has shortcomings, leaving room for owners to personalize and enhance the car to their taste. Some owners choose to build a "power car" concentrating on cranking as much horsepower out of a 5.0 as they can get, chasing quicker quarter-mile times. Others prefer to focus on stiffening the Mustang platform, bolting on bigger brakes and better rolling stock in search of race-car-like handling. Some go strictly for style. A rare few are successful at all of them. How-

Classic Design Concepts was the first to offer this rear roll style bar, much in the style of the one used on the 1968 Shelby GT500 KR convertible. They also manufacture their own line of rocker-panel exhaust systems, side scoops, and fiberglass hoods, as seen on this Cobra convertible. Note the hard tonneau cover over the convertible top area. *Classic Design Concepts*

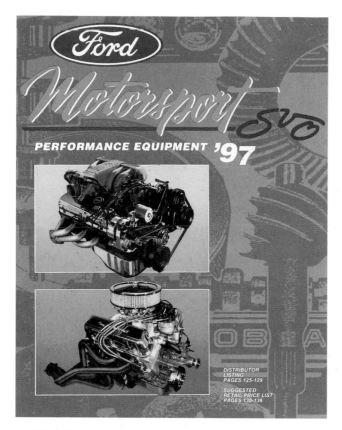

PERFORMANCE EQUIPMENT '97

DISTRIBUTOR
LISTING
PAGES 125-129

SUGGESTED
RETAIL PRICE LIST
PAGES 130-136

Ford has its own aftermarket parts provider in the form of Special Vehicle Operations. The Ford Motorsport SVO catalog is the place to start when looking to increase the performance of any late-model Ford product. The catalog includes pure racing parts, street-legal hardware, and appearance accessories. Ford also has separate catalogs for clothing and other automobilia-type goodies. *Special Vehicle Operations*

The hardware shown on this SVO display board will do wonders for the performance of any 5.0-liter V-8. At left are the GT40 upper and lower intake system as well as a set of matching heads. The Mustang's 2.73 or 3.0 ring-and-pinion is most commonly swapped out for a 3.55-ratio unit; drag racers usually start with 3.73 rear gears and get the 4.0 gears for really serious strip work. *Matt Stone*

ever, there are some Mustangs out there that look, go, stop, ride, and handle as well as some very expensive exotic cars.

In spite of the 1957 Chevy analogy, the performance aftermarket that developed around the late-model Mustangs eclipses the classic mid-1950s Chevrolets. As of this writing, there are *seven* different specialty magazines devoted strictly to Mustang and Ford performance—with four of them being Mustang-only titles. Pick up any one of them, and you'll see a hundred different companies advertising specially developed wares to make your Mustang faster, handle better, etc. It is certainly the enthusiasm of these magazines, aftermarket firms, and their customers that kept the Mustang from becoming a Probe in 1988.

Ford is unique in that it is a major player in the aftermarket as well, more so than the other American manufacturers. Through its Special Vehicle Operations

(SVO) function, Ford is both the factory and an aftermarket source of performance componentry.

Formed in the early 1980s, SVO accomplished several things. It brought a factory emphasis (and blessing) to the company's motorsports activities. It allowed the development of a special production model, the SVO Mustang. And it created an outlet for racing and street-performance parts and accessories to be sold to the public through Ford dealers.

The first SVO/Ford Motorsports performance catalog came out in 1984, and since then it has become the bible for building any hot Ford, but most particularly a Mustang. Enthusiasts eagerly await the release of each new catalog. More than just a parts source, it's also filled with tech tips, specifications, charts, and even a bit of Ford performance history.

Steeda is one of the larger players in the Mustang aftermarket business. Besides offering an extensive line of parts and accessories, Steeda builds its own line of tuner specials. Unlike many, Steeda stays away from bodywork add-ons and concentrates on cost-effective upgrades for the engine and suspension. Founder Dario Orlando has also been quite influential in supporting Mustang racers who compete with Cobra R models in the IMSA Grand Sport series. *Steeda Autosports*

American Sunroof Corporation tried offering an unusual version of the Mustang or Capri called the ASC McLaren. The body redesign turned a Mustang coupe into a two-seater convertible with a hard tonneau cover. The interior was spiced up with some tacked on wood accents, though no performance mods were made beneath the hood. Though ASC tried to play off the racing heritage of the McLaren name, and did the usual "serial number limited-edition run" type of marketing, most enthusiasts recognized that the McLaren Mustang was little more than a high-priced body kit. They are of only moderate interest today, not nearly as collectible as the Saleen or SVT Mustang variants. *Matt Stone*

orla Industries is a leader in the development of high-quality exhaust systems. This side-exhaust system was developed specially for the SN-95 Mustang and is now sold as an official SVO offering. It uses all stainless-steel tubing and mufflers plus the special rocker panels required for the installation. While dyno tests show no performance gains in this particular system (due to the bends and U-turns the pipes take), the sound is deep, and the look appeals to a lot of people. *Borla Industries*

Jack Roush made a name for himself and his companies in developing Ford race cars and engines, even helping build some factory products like the 1995 Cobra R. In 1996 Roush began offering his own brand of aftermarket parts and tuner cars. *Scott Mead*

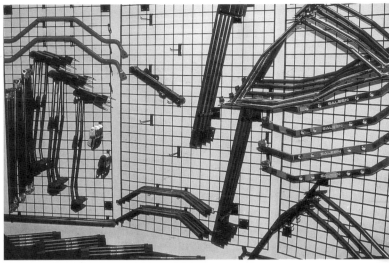

One exceptionally tricky Roush piece is this fresh-air intake system. The package includes a replacement fiberglass hood that draws cold air into the air filter at the high-pressure area located at the base of the windshield. The air is drawn through the air filter and into the upper intake. This system has been dyno-tested to produce a better-than-40-horsepower increase on a completely stock 5.0-liter V-8 and really wakes up when the cam and heads are upgraded as well. *Matt Stone*

The Fox Mustangs need help in the chassis-stiffening department, so the aftermarket has come up with all sorts of strut-tower braces, subframe connector bars, and other devices to tighten-up the chassis. A car with a stiffer chassis demonstrates more precise handling, sharper steering response, and, believe it or not, will last longer because the body experiences less fatigue from age and twisting. Though the SN-95 cars are structurally stiffer than the earlier Mustangs, they too can benefit from these handling aids. These are Saleen Performance pieces; a dozen different companies build chassis parts for late-model Mustangs. *Matt Stone*

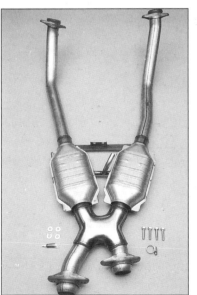

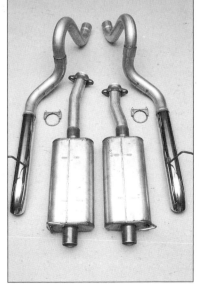

After wheels and tires, exhaust systems are the next most popular item to bolt to 5.0 or 4.6 Mustangs. A well-done exhaust adds horsepower, gas mileage, looks, and that good rumbling V-8 sound. The old days of a couple of glasspacks dumping out in front of the rear axle should be long gone; this well-engineered and smog-legal system from Bassani includes high-flow catalytic converters and large polished tailpipes. *Bassani*

SVO's mission is simple. According to Lee Hamkins of SVO, its purpose is to "develop quality performance parts and accessories for the enthusiast buyer." Hamkins said SVO's business has grown, with annual sales of approximately $30 million reached in 1997. This is no "loss leader" project for Ford either. It has to make sense from a business standpoint. Hamkins said each new part undertaken has to show some profit potential for the company. This keeps Ford stockholders happy and ensures SVO's future.

About 50 percent of the camshafts, heads, engine blocks, headers, valve covers, fuel injectors, rods, and hundreds of other components sold through the SVO

Superchargers are a popular power boost for 5.0-liter Ford V-8s. Powerdyne, Paxton, Kenne-Bell, Vortech, Whipple, and others offer them in kit form to make the installation a bit less arduous. A well-researched and well-developed kit should include all the brackets, manifolding, and hardware necessary to do the job. This particularly sanitary installation involves a B & M supercharger unit. *Matt Stone*

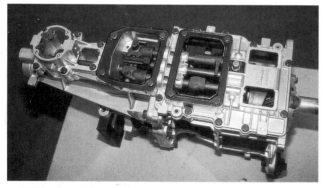

The Borg-Warner T-5 and its variants that have appeared in Mustang V-8 cars since 1983 are good transmissions, but they are somewhat limited in the amount of torque they can handle. Some Mustangers have chosen to use this Tremec five-speed transmission, which has proven to be as bullet-proof as they come. It's used in supercharged 351-powered Saleen Mustangs and was also found on the 1995 Cobra R model. *Matt Stone*

Cervini can make your Mustang look like anything from a Trans-Am racer to the Batmobile. Several companies offer ground-effects bodywork, spoilers, wings, and other parts allowing the owner to make his or her Mustang a bit different than all the rest. *Cervini*

catalog are manufactured by Ford; the other half are made under license by outside suppliers, though they carry Ford part numbers, quality assurance, and warranties just the same. This mix varies from year to year.

Even though Mustang's performance attributes will be built around an overhead-cam future, the old 5.0 is far from being put to pasture. The last factory-offered 5.0 Mustang was the 1995 GT, yet according to Hamkins, SVO's development of 5.0-related hardware continues. "If we can justify demand for a new 5.0 part, and it can be built and sold at acceptable cost and profit numbers, we'll build it," he noted.

But moreover, the aftermarket is about innovative ideas. Innovation arises from many sources including backyard enthusiasts and outside companies large and small. Some of those who spurred the development of Mustang go-fast parts in the early to mid-1980s include familiar names like Chris Kaufmann, J. Bittle, Kenny Brown, Steve Saleen, Dario Orlando, Gene Deputy, and "Stormin' Norman." Most are still involved today. There is considerable participation by individuals and companies that pre-date the Mustang era or make parts for other cars as well. Companies like Edelbrock, Borla, Hooker, Hurst, and Crane are among the many contributors. Besides the early pioneers and the established names, so many companies built their business and reputation around the Mustang only, such as BBK, Pro-5.0, and many, many others. Even Jack Roush, the supreme Mustang race car builder, has joined the fray with a line of aftermarket performance parts and accessories for the street.

Though the focus for now remains on the 5.0-liter and 351 Windsor variants, the overhead-cam movement is beginning to catch on. Turbo and supercharged applications are producing some serious horsepower; if you want a 400-horsepower Mustang, it's as easy as bolting a supercharger onto a DOHC Cobra 4.6 V-8 and hitting the highway. So far, the pushrod crowd is hanging on, but then again it took a while for the hot-rodding establishment of the 1950s to let go of Ford flatheads too. Nitrous oxide, ram air, even special blocks and heads are under continuous development. Although the handling potential of the SN-95 is still being developed, it will

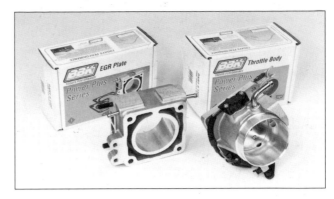

BBK is the leader in developing higher-performance fuel-injector throttle bodies and EGR plates. These pieces help open the flow of air into the upper intake manifold. This equipment is for a 5.0-liter V-8. The 4.6-liter parts are under development. *BBK*

undoubtedly yield Mustangs that will out-handle even the most radical of Fox-platform cars.

Mustang and the aftermarket are a revolving cycle; the aftermarket exists because of the Mustang, and yet the Mustang survived and flourishes today partly because of an enthusiastic aftermarket. Hopefully the fertile minds of racers, engineers, tinkerers—and Ford, in the form of SVO—will continue burning the proverbial midnight oil, working that part or goodie that will make their Mustang go just that much faster.

Another pioneer of the Mustang aftermarket was Kenny Brown. Brown now markets a line of special-edition Mustangs and Explorers in addition to a long list of aftermarket performance parts. Like Steeda, Brown focuses on performance and suspension upgrades, with only mild exterior touches to set his cars apart. This 1986 model is called the Kenny Brown Cobra C-4. *Project Industries.*

# Track

## By Patrick C. Paternie

Mustang racing fans didn't have a lot to cheer about during the latter part of the 1970s as their favorite car suffered from both an energy and an identity crisis on and off the track. This lasted through 1981 when their faith was restored by an advertising headline that was simple and to the point. "The Boss is back" was how Ford announced to the world that it had unleashed the first 5.0 Mustang GT in 1982. The ads were a warning directed primarily toward the buyers of high-performance street machines but proved to be prophetic for racers as the original pony car soon began reasserting itself on the nation's race tracks, a trend that grew stronger throughout the rest of the 1980s when the Mustang was the "prancing horse" of choice in GT sports car racing. In the 1990s Mustang racing continued to expand and diversify, creating its own special niches like drag racing 5.0 shoot-outs.

Whether by coincidence or design, the Boss was back just in time to take advantage of rules changes in Trans-Am racing. After spending most of the 1970s as a series dominated by imported sports cars like Porsches and Jaguars along with exotic variants of the Corvette, in 1980 the Trans-Am returned to its roots with a weight/displacement rules formula that allowed tube-frame chassis construction as long as the cars retained a stock appearance. While Porsches, Nissans, and Corvettes still ruled during the early years of this formula, in 1983 the series was dominated by a pair of DeAtley Camaros, basically road racing versions of short-track stock cars, driven by David Hobbs and

Ford's racing fortunes really took off in the mid-1980s when Bob Riley began building Trans-Am and IMSA cars. Tom Gloy won the T-A championship with a Riley-built car in 1984, and Riley-built cars racked up lots of wins over the next decade. This is an IMSA GTO machine piloted by future Trans-Am champ and CART regular Scott Pruett and former Olympian Bruce Jenner. The site is Riverside International Raceway in 1986. *Matt Stone*

Not all the cars competed as Mustangs. Many T-A and GTO racers were trimmed-out as Capris to spread the wealth to that nameplate and the Lincoln-Mercury dealers who so badly needed a performance image boost. *Matt Stone*

Willy T. Ribbs. That spurred Ford's racing crew into action. Pony car racing was back, and it didn't take long for Ford to respond.

Tom Gloy was the first to race a Mustang in the reborn Trans-Am. The 1979 Formula Atlantic champion had an inauspicious debut at the fourth race of the 1981 season when he finished 46th at Road Atlanta. Things got better as the season progressed with a third place result at Trois-Rivieres. The first win for Gloy and Mustang came at Sears Point in the season finale. Racing in only six of nine races, Gloy still managed to accumulate enough points for the season to rank ninth overall in the standings.

In 1982 Gloy set a qualifying record at Mid-Ohio and, in a case of déja vu, won the last race of the season at Sears Point. A year of development made his Mustang much more competitive in the other eight races that year giving him a fourth place in the season championship points total. Rob McFarlin's sixth place in the championship points put two Mustangs in the top 10.

Gloy added Lyn St. James to his team in 1983 to battle the DeAtley Camaro duo of Hobbs and Ribbs. He also switched bodywork to resemble the Mercury Capri, which was essentially a Mustang GT wearing a suit tailored by Lincoln-Mercury. Although he never won a race during the 12-race season, by consistently finishing third to the DeAtley steamroller attack and occasionally second when misfortune struck one of the Camaros, Gloy actually led the championship points race going into the

# Pro 5.0 and Other Mustang Shootouts

It all started with a guy named Stormin' Norman Gray who drove a red, white, and blue Mustang convertible that could turn 9 seconds in the quarter-mile at events like Bill Alexander's Fun Ford Weekends in the late 1980s. That's the way Ken Holcomb of Holcomb Motorsports remembers the early days of Pro 5.0 and modified street Mustang racing that was dedicated to seeing how fast a Mustang with a 5.0-liter block and a stock-bodied chassis could be peddled down a drag strip.

Holcomb has built a successful business selling high-performance parts to Mustang owners who may not all be building 8-second machines in their backyards but certainly are caught up in the excitement of racing late-model Mustangs. Holcomb's Lumberton, North Carolina-based company helps spread this excitement by staging two events a year at Rockingham Dragway. The "5.0 Civil War" pits the fastest 5.0s north of the Mason-Dixon Line against those from the south. "Fast Fords in the Fall" is open to all Ford drivers. Even Stormin' Norman puts on his own event, the Stormin' Norman Invitational at Maple Grove Raceway in Pennsylvania.

"It's almost to the level of the Chevrolet now," says Holcomb about the diversity of parts available these days for late-model Mustangs. Holcomb has sold high-performance Ford parts for about 25 years.

The basic concept that draws the crowds to these all-Mustang shootouts involves match races to see who has the fastest "streetable" late-model Mustang. But over the years a number of classes evolved based on weight, engine size, and modifications. While Pro 5.0 stretches the definition of what is "streetable" in pursuit of 7-second elapsed times (big blocks have replaced 5.0-derived motors, and tube frames have replaced the back half of the chassis), the Outlaw 5.0 class sticks to the concept of a full-bodied car with a stock design chassis and a 5.0-liter engine block. Thanks to technology and performance parts development, the Outlaw cars can produce close to 600 horsepower before hitting the nitrous bottle. They are capable of 9-second dashes down the drag strip. The use of "Power Adders" separates the purists—who shun the use of nitrous, turbos, or superchargers and any combinations thereof to make more horsepower—from those who'll do whatever it takes to get down in the 8-second category. The purists, on the other hand, are doggedly chipping away at the 11-second bracket.

That's the appeal of the sport. The popularity of late-model Mustang drag racing is not so much a case of building cars that conform to a formula or strict set of rules. It's a whole lot simpler than that. It's about people who love Mustangs and express that love by making their cars go as fast as they can.

---

final two races to be held at Riverside and the parking lot of Caesar's Palace in Las Vegas. He again finished third at Las Vegas, but it was too late, as a 26th place in the Riverside event handed the title to Hobbs. Ribbs finished five points ahead of Gloy to become runner-up to Hobbs. St. James contributed three top-10 finishes during the year to put the other Capri in the 10th spot in the final championship points tally.

Ford got serious about Trans-Am racing in 1984, giving Jack Roush a simple game plan when he joined the series—just win, baby. Roush responded by building the Roush-Prototab Capris for Tom Gloy and Greg Pickett. Roush had already established a reputation within the Dearborn automaker's walls as a guy who not only knew how to make Fords fly, he knew how to make them win. And winning, especially against Chevrolet, was what racing Fords was all about. Roush took the new SVO four-bolt main block, a descendant of the BOSS 302, added a set of SVO aluminum heads along with an 830-cfm Holley carb to give Gloy and Pickett

A Mustang in name only, the Mustang GTP was a front-engined, turbocharged four-cylinder racer that competed in the top IMSA GTP (Grand Touring Prototype) class during 1984 and 1985. Although these Mustangs placed first and second in their 1984 debut at Road America, they achieved little success thereafter. The car was very fast, but the engine was over-stressed and suffered reliability problems. It's seen here in 1985 with Klaus Ludwig and Bobby Rahal teamed as pilots. *Matt Stone*

The Roush Team SCCA Trans-Am entry at Riverside Raceway in 1984 was driven by Greg Pickett. In long-distance IMSA races, Pickett was often teamed with Willy T. Ribbs who went on to become a big winner in Trans-Am and ultimately drove Indy Cars. *Matt Stone*

550-plus horsepower to chase down the new DeAtley Corvettes. Bob Riley, SVO's ace chassis man who has gone on to form the Riley & Scott team that developed a championship winning IMSA WSC sports car, saw to it that the Capri suspension package would put all of Roush's SVO power tricks to good use.

Carrying 7-Eleven sponsorship, Gloy won three races and finished second six times to rack up 225 points for a convincing run to the Trans-Am championship. Pickett won four races and finished second in the points. Further revenge was inflicted for the Camaro power play of 1983 by having a third Roush Capri complete a hat trick of the top three places in the championship. To

make things even sweeter, it was driven by Willy T. Ribbs who had left the DeAtley team after the first race of the 1984 season when he was involved in a fistfight with another competitor. After sitting out the season's initial four races, Ribbs won four times during 1984 for Roush.

The highlight of the 1984 season was a clean sweep led by Gloy in the Trans-Am race that accompanied the running of the Detroit Grand Prix. Winning convincingly at home, before both Ford and Chevrolet executives,

W hat better way to test the performance of all those new go-fast and handle-better parts than to put the car on the track? Mustang club races are extremely popular, and these two Fox-bodied cars were photographed while participating in a Cobra club event at Willow Springs Raceway. Letting a car stretch its legs on the track is big-time fun, but many Mustang owners rendered their cars unstreetable by going all-out in the modifications department. A simple solution is to build one for the track and keep another slightly less radical Mustang around for the commute to work. *Matt Stone*

probably ranked as high as winning the season championship in some corporate quarters. Even a guest drive by Michael Andretti in one of the DeAtley cars didn't stop Roush's march to the top three spots. Thanks to Gloy and Roush, the Boss definitely was back, albeit as a Mercury Capri.

The Roush roller coaster continued the next season. John Jones and Wally Dallenbach Jr. were Gloy's new teammates in 1985. Dallenbach went on to win the championship that year before defecting to Chevrolet in 1986. The Capris also retired from Ford Motorsport after the 1985 season. They were replaced by the XR4Ti Merkur that would carry the Mercury banner in the Trans-Am from 1986 through 1988.

Meanwhile, Mustangs dressed as Mustangs were becoming the scourge of IMSA GTO racing. It started when Roush won the 1984 season finale. Jones and Dallenbach, in addition to their Trans-Am duties, also competed in the

1985 IMSA series with a pair of very loud and very fast 600-plus-horsepower Motorcraft-sponsored Mustangs. Lyn St. James and Willy Ribbs also drove Roush Mustangs, while Darin Brassfield drove the Brooks Racing 7-Eleven Thunderbird, another Roush creation. The 19-year-old Jones won eight races to become the class champion, his only competition coming from fellow teammates who ended up second (Brassfield), third (Dallenbach), and fifth (St. James). The season-opener in 1985 was the 24 Hours of Daytona, where the Mustang driven by Dallenbach, Jones, and Doc Bundy captured GTO class honors. It was to be the first of nine consecutive 24-hour wins at Daytona for Roush cars. Ford's domination of the 1985 IMSA season also led to winning its first manufacturer's championship since 1970 when another Jones boy, by the name of Parnelli, drove a Mustang to the Trans-Am title.

A Roush Mustang was the mount of the 1986 IMSA GTO champ. This time the honors went to Scott Pruett

# Tommy Kendall Trans-Am King

During the 1997 SCCA Trans-Am season, Tom Kendall whipped out an eraser and wiped the Trans-Am record book clean. The top numbers for total wins, most consecutive wins (11 as of this writing), and the most Trans-Am championships all belong to the tall, blonde, California native. Most convincing of all was Kendall's "Threepeat" performance of taking the Trans-Am title crown in 1995, 1996, and 1997 (the first of his four T-A titles came in 1990). The three most recent titles and all those checkered flags came at the wheel of a Roush-built-and-entered Mustang Cobra Trans-Am racer. His accomplishments finally eclipsed the records of the late Mark Donahue who did his record-setting in a Chevrolet Camaro. One of the most memorable victories came in the 1995 Rolex 24-Hour Enduro where he teamed with NASCAR standout Mark Martin, journalist Michael Brockman, and driver/actor Paul Newman to win the GT class . . . in a Roush Mustang, of course.

It hasn't all been roses, however. There have been grievous injuries to his feet and legs, less than successful NASCAR tryouts, and seasons without a ride. But the good-natured and well-spoken Kendall comes back a bit stronger each time and has his eyes firmly set on a top open-wheel CART or IRL ride. At barely 32 (as of this writing), he has notched nine various SCCA professional and IMSA championships.

I spoke to Kendall to get his views on racing, the Trans-Am series, his team, and Mustangs in general. Here are some excerpts from that interview:

Author: What is a Mustang Trans-Am car like to drive?

Kendall: I got to do a neat thing last year with [1970 Trans-Am champion] Parnelli Jones at the Ford Proving Grounds. I got to take a spin in, I believe, a 1966 Mustang, one of the first Trans-Am cars. Its amazing how they've evolved. Obviously, that began as a street car and had modifications done. Now, we're at the point where it is totally purpose-built, tube frame; they've tried to keep the identity by having the body rules [which require certain areas of the car to resemble a production Mustang]. Parnelli just raved about the new car, and for obvious reasons. It's quite sophisticated, but it still has the character of a Mustang . . . it's probably the most fun formula in racing, in my mind . . . if someone gave you a Mustang and said, "unlimited budged, so go to town," my car is probably what you'd end up with. They do everything well. They have 640 horsepower now. They stop on a dime with the huge brake rotors we have now. But they're not artificially fast like a high-downforce ground-effects car. So the experience is just like your wildest dreams of what a street car could be . . . and then just a little bit more.

Author: Maybe the ultimate "tuner car"?

Kendall: Yes. That's the appeal . . . there still is a strong visual identity. When I look at the car, I think, "That's the ultimate tuner car." It's as low as you can get it. It's as wide as you can get it. It's just trick, and that gets my blood pumping. To get to drive it, I kinda have to pinch myself. I started as an enthusiast like everybody else, and now, you can lose sight of the fact that while you're getting there, how far you've come, then all of a sudden I realize I drive the baddest factory Mustang race car in the world. Every time I look at it I'll say, "That is such a bad ride."

**Author:** How much better is your Mustang versus a Trans-Am Camaro [perhaps an obvious question given Kendall's run of 11 straight wins]?

**Kendall:** Fortunately, the Mustang seems to be a little bit better! It all has to do with the groups that are behind it really; my whole group that was with me [this year] has been with me my whole career. We were able to keep refining it, whereas Chevrolet has stopped their support. It's logical that the guys still working at it are going to be a little better.

**Author:** Congratulations on the 1997 season and breaking so many records this year. What does that feel like?

**Kendall:** The consecutive win record was the biggest one we broke, and we were lucky enough to break a lot of records this year, but that one was a record that had resided in the Chevy camp for 30 years. I get a lot more comments along those lines from Ford guys who have had to put up with that [Donohue's] darn Sunoco Camaro and hear about it for 30 years, which is what makes our accomplishment that much more special. By virtue of the fact that it stood for so long, it was obviously a very significant and meaningful record.

**Author:** What is it like driving for Jack Roush?

**Kendall:** His mark is all over the place, but our deal has kind of been our own little unit. In a lot of ways it was perfect, as he provided us with all the tools that we needed. It was up to us to figure out which ones they were and how to implement them. We had the resources, but we were allowed to do things however we wanted. It's the ultimate situation.

**Author:** Do you own a Mustang?

**Kendall:** I do. It's the only one I've owned. I have a '95 Cobra R, #248 of the 250. It only has about 120 miles on it. I've taken it [cruising] to Bob's Big Boy in Toluca Lake a few times, but other than that I want to keep it pristine. My dad has an '84 SVO; he raced a couple of different Mustangs. My Trans-Am debut was actually in an ex-Tom Gloy car in 1987. It was the car he won the championship with in 1984. We owned it, and I drove it at Long Beach in '87. I think I'm going to end up buying that from my dad. I started my career in that car, and he had some history with it too. There are a few Mustangs in the family.

**Author:** Any final thoughts?

**Kendall:** One of my very first racing heroes was Klaus Ludwig. I saw him race the Zakspeed Mustang at Sears Point in the early 1980s. I've been in love with that car ever since. That was my first Mustang racing memory; not as nostalgic as watching the Bud Moore cars run in the 1970s, as I was only four years old at the time. I have a healthy appreciation for the early cars that started it all. If I had my eye on another Mustang to own, it would be a '70 with a big block!

The 1992 Trans-Am action at Detroit was as good as it got. Chevrolet, Ford, and Dodge all participated with factory support. Dodge backed out shortly after this race to sponsor the IROC series, and Chevrolet ended their factory support at the end of the 1996 season. This left Ford as the only factory-supported effort for 1997. *Matt Stone*

who had 7 wins and 9 pole positions in 17 races. In 34 races over the 1985 and 1986 seasons, Roush cars won 17 times! From 1984 to 1989, Roush also had 46 Trans-Am victories, which was more wins than the rest of the competitors combined.

For 1988 Roush's IMSA GTO efforts were run under the Lincoln-Mercury banner. The Merkur XR4Ti was the model of choice, but at certain races, like the Daytona and Sebring enduros, re-bodied Mustang V-8s were also entered based on their reliability record. Drivers who competed in V-8 cars for Roush at Sebring and Daytona during the 1980s were people like Kyle Petty, Ken Schrader, Bill Elliott, and Ricky Rudd.

The biggest differences between the V-8 cars that Roush ran in the Trans-Am and in IMSA GTO was that the more restrictive rules of the Trans-Am regarding bodywork and tire and wheel size made the IMSA cars about 2 seconds a lap faster. The four-cylinder turbo cars that Roush campaigned alongside the V-8s in IMSA enjoyed a 100-horsepower advantage over the more traditional American powerplants that pumped out around 600 ponies. Turbo lag and a higher stress factor

that could affect reliability were what the fours conceded to make that additional power.

The Mustang observed its 25th anniversary in 1989. What better way to celebrate than by returning to the Trans-Am. A special silver-anniversary Mustang was prepared. The driver was to become a name associated with Mustang racing of the 1990s as much as Jones and Follmer were in the late 1960s and early 1970s. Dorsey Schroeder won half of the 14 races that year driving the red, white, and blue 25th Anniversary Mustang that wore, appropriately, the number 25 on its flanks. He also finished sixth or better in the races he didn't win with the exception of one DNF at Cleveland. The prettiest Mustang in 1989, however, was the black and gold JPS-sponsored car of Robert Lappalainen who finished fifth in the standings. Ron Fellows also drove a Roush Mustang in 1989. Appropriately, the Canadian took the Mackenzie Financial Services car to a win at Mosport Park. Lyn St. James finished ninth in the season's standings to put her Mustang in the top 10 overall. When the smoke cleared, the 1989 Trans-Am season turned out to be a year-long gala affair to commemorate the Mustang's 25th birthday.

" "V-8s are great straight" is an old saw that still plays true. Mustangs are popular at bracket racing and "run what you brung" events, as well as some of the more serious drag racing series designed specifically for Mustangs, particularly 5.0 cars. Several of the Ford magazines organize "Mustang Shootouts" just for this purpose, and the country is crawling with cars that will run below 10 seconds. *SUPER FORD*

The party was over in 1990 when Tom Kendall, driving for Chevrolet, captured six victories to win the Trans-Am driver's championship. Robby Gordon won the 1992 Long Beach Grand Prix Trans-Am race, but it wasn't until 1993 that Ford had something special to celebrate as Gloy Racing opened the season with three straight victories. Ron Fellows was the victor at Long Beach and Road Atlanta while Dorsey Schroeder took his Mustang to victory circle at the always important Detroit race.

The 1994 Trans-Am season kicked off with its first-ever visit to Miami. Tom Kendall was the flag-to-flag victor as Roush Racing became the first team in Trans-Am history to pile up 50 wins. The past also proved to be a prologue as to how Kendall and Roush planned to help Ford race into the future. The combo was good enough with a more than able assist from Gloy Racing's five victories to help Ford capture the manufacturer's title that year even though ex-Ford driver Scott Pruett drove a Camaro to the driver's championship. Dorsey Schroeder posted three wins for the Gloy team, while the fast and exciting Boris Said III earned a spot in Mustang racing annals by snatching a last-lap win from Kendall at Road America.

In 1995 the tables were turned as Kendall won the driver's championship while Chevrolet took the manufacturer's honors. Schroeder had three wins and Said another as Tom Gloy's independent Mustang team held its own against the Roush factory effort. Ron Fellows had deserted the Ford camp for a ride with Chevrolet, and a season-long battle, punctuated by some controversial incidents with Kendall, added even more spice to the simmering stew shared by Ford and Chevy competitors. Another obstacle in Kendall's path to the series top slot was the rule instituted by the SCCA to invert the starting position of the top five qualifiers in order to create more passing situations. This obviously worked against Kendall who, despite being the fastest on a number of occasions, became only the second driver in Trans-Am history to win the driver's crown with only one victory. Kendall and his Roush Mustang would make up for that soon enough.

Ford Mustang Cobras helped the Trans-Am celebrate its 30th anniversary in 1996 with strong performances throughout the year by Kendall, Schroeder, and Said. In the end, Kendall posted four wins to take the

Sometimes its hard to tell where the Street 5.0 ends and the race car begins. Many race organizations insist that the Mustang's basic unibody structure remain intact, in order for a car to compete in a "Street 5.0" Catagory. *SUPER FORD*

driver's championship, while Ford snatched the manufacturer's cup back from Chevy.

Roush and Kendall still had a point to make, and they did it resoundingly in 1997. Kendall broke Mark Donohue's long-standing record of 8 consecutive Trans-Am wins by taking 11 in a row before finishing second to the Mustang of Mike Borkowski, the 1997 Rookie of the Year. Kendall was the fast qualifier but had to start fifth in compliance with Trans-Am rules. Borkowski started on the pole and was determined not to give up the lead. Kendall, who had been tapped from the rear by Dorsey Schroeder and spun off, charged from 17th position to catch Borkowski with 30 laps to go. The rookie never gave in. On the last lap he drove completely off course in the fourth turn at Pikes Peak International Raceway but recovered the lead as he slid back on track and tapped Kendall out of the way. Kendall came back to finish second by 10.45 seconds.

In IMSA the Roush Mustang/Capri juggernaut established its own 10-race winning streak as a GTS victory at the 1995 24 Hours of Daytona kept alive the streak started at that event in 1985. Mark Martin partnered with Tom Kendall for the victory, but it was the car's sponsor and third driver who stole the show. Veteran racer/actor/director Paul Newman celebrated his 70th birthday by carrying his share of the driving chores with the two Roush drivers. The car carried the name of Newman's latest movie, *Nobody's Fool*, as a sponsor. Both Newman and Roush could lay claim to that title when the 24 hours was up.

The Mustang was also sowing its oats in other racing series sanctioned by the SCCA and IMSA. SCCA began a Professional Showroom Stock Endurance Racing Series in 1984 that has seen a variety of sponsors over the years including *Playboy* magazine and Escort radar detectors.

One constant has been the dominance of Mustang GTs, especially the ones that have been massaged by Saleen Autosport. Steve Saleen has employed a number of drivers associated with Mustang racing history in his championship-winning cars, the most notable being George Follmer and Parnelli Jones in 1987.

Success hasn't come as quickly to Mustang drivers over the years in IMSA's Endurance Championship series. It took 12 years before a Cobra "R" sponsored by Steeda Autosports and driven by the team of Boris Said and Shawn Hendricks won a six-hour event at Texas World Speedway in May 1996. The Steeda team repeated that victory at Mosport in August 1996. In 1997 Said and Hendricks won the season opener at Daytona where three other Steeda-sponsored Cobra Rs took second, fourth, and fifth. One of the team's most promising new members was Jason Priestley of *Beverly Hills 90210* fame.

Another television star who is making his mark racing Mustangs is "tool man" Tim Allen. Allen and Steve Saleen established the Saleen/Allen "RRR" Speedlab team in 1995 to compete in the SCCA's World Challenge Sports class against Porsche, Lotus, Viper, BMW, and, of course, the Corvette. Allen admits to living out a high school fantasy by carrying on a Ford versus Chevy grudge match pitting his 500-plus-horsepower Saleen Mustang SR against the plastic Chevy sports car. By winning two of the nine events and placing well in the rest, the team won the class championship in 1996.

Saleen also made Mustang history overseas by entering two of his highly modified Mustangs in the GT-2 class for the 24 Hours of Le Mans. They were the first Mustangs at LeMans in 30 years. Running in a class dominated by Porsches and that also included a quartet of Vipers and the Callaway Corvette LM, the car, driven by Saleen, Price Cobb, and Carlos Palau, qualified a respectable third in class behind the factory Viper team. The other Saleen car was seventh fastest. Unfortunately electrical problems struck that car early into the race. The Saleen/Cobb/Palau car soldiered on through the night despite gearbox problems, only to drop out around 9 A.M. the next day when the left rear suspension collapsed. The car still was a ninth-place finisher in its class.

A major part of the Mustang's appeal has always been its adaptability to meet the demands of world-class professional racers while also serving the grass-roots racing needs of weekend warriors. Mustangs have always been competitive at the regional and national levels of SCCA's amateur racing programs. The American Sedan class is a popular battleground where 5.0-liter Mustangs from 1979 and up battle

This Nevada Highway Patrol "Chaser" drag car was intended to prove that law enforcement officers can be racing (and Mustang) enthusiasts. This Mustang was part of an educational program that began in 1989, focusing on impaired driving with school-age children. The Pro-Chassis-built car began life as a 1989 Mustang. Now it packs a 598-cubic-inch Ford SVO big-block V-8. Backed by a Lenco pro-stock style transmission, its best quarter-mile time was a 7.61. The car was retired in 1997, and the Nevada Highway Patrol donated it to the Imperial Palace Auto Collection. *Imperial Palace*

late-model Camaros in a series where the rules are very similar to those of the original Trans-Am in the 1960s. For racers who prefer battling the bow-tie brigade in a full-on tube-frame racer that bears a faint resemblance to a Mustang, there is the more exotic GT1 category.

Of course, there is another group of Mustang enthusiasts who take a more direct approach to racing—like how fast you can go in a straight line. Rickie Smith was the IHRA Pro Stock World Champion for most of the 1980s running huge "mountain motors" of 655 cubic inches or more that powered his stock-appearing Mustangs through the quarter-mile in 7 seconds with speeds above 180 miles per hour. Even more impressive is what has happened since then thanks to an increasing group of hard-core 5.0 fanatics that have pushed the envelope for stock-bodied cars from 10-second passes through the quarter to times that would make even Rickie Smith flinch at the line. From Pro 5.0 to Outlaw 5.0, more and more all-Mustang drag racing meets are taking place around the country.

As Ford warned in 1982, The Boss definitely is back. It has won enough championships over the last 15 years to prove it and, judging by all the racing activity currently going on, should be around for a long time to come.

## MUSTANG MUSINGS

There are many Mustang books, but most of them cover the 1964 1/2–1973 models or run the gamut from 1964 1/2 through today. But there are few, mostly of the performance-related variety, that give good coverage, or even emphasis, to the Fox and FOX-4 cars. Here are a few that I recommend:

*Mustang,* by Randy Leffingwell. Though this volume reaches back to the Mustang's beginnings, it gives more than adequate treatment to the late-model cars. Leffingwell's prose is easy to read, and his photography is outstanding. A good, all-around look at the cars if you don't want to get too caught up in the restoration and option minutia. Currently in print.

*Mustang Performance Handbook and Mustang Performance Handbook 2,* by William R. Mathis. Covers all manner of modifications and performance upgrades, focusing on late-model Mustangs only. You'd need 1,000 copies of the various Mustang-related magazines to get this much information. The only problem with these books is that they were dated the day they were printed as the aftermarket develops new hardware so quickly. Most of the information is for 5.0 cars. Currently in print.

*Saleen: The History and Development of the Saleen Mustang,* by Patty Redeker. The title tells it all, and this small, black and white volume does a good job at getting you up to speed on Saleen and his cars. It covers cars through 1993 and the pre-Saleen-Allen racing endeavors. This book has a bit of a public relations ring to it, but all the specs and information on the pre-FOX-4 cars are worth having. Currently in print.

*The 5.0 Liter Mustang Bolt-On Performance Guide,* by John Smith. Smith is an experienced Ford hot rodder and writer, and this volume serves as a good performance parts and accessories buyers' guide. There's not a lot of how-to or step-by-step, but Smith covers most of the different parts and systems out there. No overhead-camshafts fans need apply as the engine sections are strictly 5.0 related, but suspension pieces and other areas do cover the newest Mustangs.

## MAGAZINES

There are more magazines dedicated to late-model Mustang and Ford high performance than for any other marque.

*5.0,* Petersen Publishing. It doesn't get any more specific than this. Though the name references the 1979–1995 cars, there's plenty of information on the 4.6 cars as well. As the earliest Fox cars are getting to be 20 years old now, this magazine gives restoration and preservation tips, as well as the latest and greatest performance mods, bolt-ons, and tests of the new Mustangs.

*Super Ford,* Dobbs Publishing. One of the best Ford "screwdriver" magazines with lots of tech. Though you will also see SHOs, FE-motored Fords, and pickups featured, the main focus is on Mustang performance and tech. A nice balance of car features, tech, how-to, new parts reviews, and editorial.

*Mustang Monthly,* Dobbs Publishing. A sister publication to *Super Ford, Mustang Monthly* is a more restoration- and originality-oriented magazine. There's a lot of emphasis on the early classic cars, but there is coverage of the late models as well. Still, if you are a Mustang person, it's a good one to read as it's 100 percent dedicated to your subject, including the newest Mustang products.

*Mustangs and Fords,* Petersen Publishing. Not as completely focused on Mustangs as *5.0,* nor as technical, but still a good all-around performance Ford book with emphasis on Mustangs.

*Muscle Mustangs and Fast Fords,* CSK Publishing. The largest and biggest-selling Mustang performance book out there. Decent tech information, very good event coverage, and lots of car features plus new products.

*Mustang Illustrated,* McMullen-Argus Publishing. Besides *5.0* and *Mustang Monthly,* the only other strictly Mustang magazine out there. *MI* is sort of a blend of the two Dobbs magazines, though from an overall quality level, it is not quite up to the Dobbs level.

*Ford Hi-Performance,* McMullen Argus Publishing. A counterpart to *Mustangs and Fords,* this one covers the overall Ford performance scene.

## WEB SITES

There are many Mustang-related web sites on the Internet, ranging from clubs and individuals, to magazines, the aftermarket, and Ford itself. Some have information of general interest, while others are catalogs and marketing tools, but a considerable amount of good information does exist at your fingertips. If you are a web enthusiast, you know that many good sites have links to others, so usually a couple are enough to get you rolling on-line. In no particular order:

*www.ford.com*
Ford's factory web site, including new product information on the latest Mustang and SVT products.

*www.corral.net*
This is a site called the Late Model Mustang Corral, and it is simply outstanding. Lots of good information, crisp graphics, calculator functions, news, a chat room, and great links to many other sites. Start here!

*www.lmmustang.com*
Similar to above, but on a smaller scale. Good editorial on late-model cars, including book reviews and drive reports.

*www.saleen.com*
Saleen Performance's site includes new product information and the latest goings-on with the race teams. Bios on Steve and the drivers, Team Saleen information, special parts deals, etc.

*www.steeda.com*
Much like Saleen's site, the steeda site offers lots of product news, specials, close-outs, and information on Mustang Cobra racing.

*www.svtcobra.com*
Official site for the SVT Cobra club.

*www.alternativeauto.com*
This is a commercial site that makes a business of selling high-tech performance accessories. Besides the usual catalog, ordering information, and the like, they put out a considerable amount of 5.0-related material and tech information. Crisp graphics.

*www.carlounge.com*
An interesting E-Zine with special sections for Mustangs and SVT Cobras.

*www.bondurant.com*
Bob Bondurant's School of High Performance driving is the only Ford-sanctioned driving and racing school to use Mustangs and SVT Cobras. The site gives all the pertinent class information plus tells about Bondurant's line of SuperFormance Cobra replicas. Though this has nothing to do with Mustangs, they are neat cars that any Ford enthusiast should enjoy.

*home.mem.net/~toddstin*
Strictly 5.0 stuff on this independently maintained site.

*www.mustangworks.com*
Another good E-Zine dedicated only to Mustangs, mostly of the late-model variety. Cars for sale, tech, chat.

*www.gate.net/~lxcoupe*
A good site for the 5.0 drag racing fan.

## MUSTANG EXPERIENCE MUSEUM

As this book was going to press, plans were well underway toward the construction of a proper historical venue dedicated to the Mustang. The movement began as a grassroots one but quickly gained momentum as people and companies important to the Mustang became involved. The Honorary Board of Directors includes Mustang luminaries such as Edsel Ford II, Jack Roush, and Steve Saleen, and fund raising continues to get the project off the ground.

An initial group of 10 cities was vying to be the museum's home, and that list was to be cut to four in late 1997 with a final selection due in the first quarter of 1998. Wherever the final spot, the group intends the grand opening to take place in April 2000, exactly 36 years after the first Mustang hit the market.

The phone number for information (as of this writing) is 888-MUST-EXP.

| Year/Model | 1982 GT 5.0 | Year/Model | 1985 GT 5.0 |
|---|---|---|---|
| MSRP | $8,965 base, $12,722 as tested | MSRP | $9,885 base, $10,974 as tested |

| **Dimensions** | | **Dimensions** | |
|---|---|---|---|
| Overall length (in) | 179.1 | Overall length (in) | 179.3 |
| Wheelbase (in) | 100.4 | Wheelbase (in) | 100.5 |
| Width (in) | 69.1 | Width (in) | 69.1 |
| Height (in) | 51.4 | Height (in) | 52.1 |
| Track (in, f/r) | 56.6/57.0 | Track (in, f/r) | 56.6/57.0 |
| Curb weight (lbs) | 3,130 | Curb weight (lbs) | 3,190 |

| **Engine** | | **Engine** | |
|---|---|---|---|
| No. of cylinders | 8 | No. of cylinders | 8 |
| Layout | 90-degree V-8, overhead valves, 2 valves per cylinder | Layout | 90-degree V-8, overhead valves, 2 valves per cylinder |
| Construction | Iron block and heads | Construction | Iron block and heads |
| Bore x stroke (in) | 4.00x3.00 | Bore x stroke (in) | 4.00x3.00 |
| Displacement (cc/ci) | 4,942/302 | Displacement (cc/ci) | 4,942/302 |
| Compression ratio | 8.3:1 | Compression ratio | 8.3:1 |
| Horsepower rating @ rpm | 157 @ 4,200 | Horsepower rating @ rpm | 210 @ 4,600 |
| Torque rating @ rpm (lb-ft) | 240 @ 2,400 | Torque rating @ rpm (lb-ft) | 265 @ 3,400 |
| Intake/carburetion | Ford 2-barrel carburetor | Intake/carburetion | Holley 4-barrel carburetor |

| **Drivetrain** | | **Drivetrain** | |
|---|---|---|---|
| Standard transmission | 4-speed manual | Standard transmission | 5-speed manual |
| Optional transmission | NA | Optional transmission | NA |
| Standard differential ratio | 3.08 | Standard differential ratio | 3.08 |

| **Chassis and Suspension** | | **Chassis and Suspension** | |
|---|---|---|---|
| Frame type | Unit body | Frame type | Unit body |
| Brake type | Power disc/drum | Brake type | Power disc/drum |
| Front suspension | Modified MacPherson strut, lower A-arm, coil springs | Front suspension | Modified MacPherson strut, lower A-arm, coil springs |
| Rear suspension | Live axle, upper and lower trailing arms, coil springs, tube shocks, anti-tramp bars | Rear suspension | Live axle, upper and lower trailing arms, coil springs, tube shocks, anti-tramp bars |
| Steering type | Rack and pinion | Steering type | Rack and pinion |
| Turns (lock to lock) | 3.1 | Turns (lock to lock) | 3.1 |
| Turning circle (ft) | 37.1 | Turning circle (ft) | 37.1 |

| **Performance** | | **Performance** | |
|---|---|---|---|
| 0–30 mph (sec) | 2.6 | 0–30 mph (sec) | 2.4 est. |
| 0–60 mph (sec) | 8.0 | 0–60 mph (sec) | 7.2 |
| 0–100 mph (sec) | 25.0 | 0–100 mph (sec) | 19.1 |
| Standing 1/4 mile (sec) | 16.3 | Standing 1/4 mile (sec) | 15.9 |
| Data source | Road & Track | Data source | Road & Track |

| Year/Model | 1987 GT 5.0 | Year/Model | 1994 GT 5.0 |
|---|---|---|---|
| MSRP | $11,324 base, $12,548 as tested | MSRP | $17,280 base, $21,500 as tested |

**Dimensions**

| | 1987 GT 5.0 | | 1994 GT 5.0 |
|---|---|---|---|
| Overall Length (in) | 179.3 | Overall length (in) | 181.5 |
| Wheelbase (in) | 100.5 | Wheelbase (in) | 101.3 |
| Width (in) | 69.1 | Width (in) | 71.8 |

**Dimensions**

| | 1987 GT 5.0 | | 1994 GT 5.0 |
|---|---|---|---|
| Height (in) | 52.1 | Height (in) | 53.1 |
| Track (in, f/r) | 56.6/57.0 | Track (in, f/r) | 60.1/58.7 |
| Curb Weight (lbs) | 3,270 | Curb weight (lbs) | 3,400 |

**Engine**

| | 1987 GT 5.0 | | 1994 GT 5.0 |
|---|---|---|---|
| No. of cylinders | 8 | No. of cylinders | 8 |
| Layout | 90-degree V-8, overhead valves, 2 valves per cylinder | Layout | 90-degree V-8, overhead valves, 2 valves per cylinder |
| Construction | Iron block and heads | Construction | Iron block and heads |
| Bore x stroke (in) | 4.00x3.00 | Bore x stroke (in) | 4.00x3.00 |
| Displacement (cc/ci) | 4,942/302 | Displacement (cc/ci) | 4,942/302 |
| Compression ratio: | 9.0:1 | Compression ratio: | 9.0:1 |
| Horsepower rating @ rpm | 225 @ 4,400 | Horsepower rating @ rpm | 215 @ 4,400 |
| Torque Rating @ rpm (lb-ft) | 300 @ 3,000 | Torque rating @ rpm (lb-ft) | 285 @ 3,400 |
| Intake/carburetion | Direct-port electronic fuel injection | Intake/carburetion | Direct-port electronic fuel injection |

**Drivetrain**

| | 1987 GT 5.0 | | 1994 GT 5.0 |
|---|---|---|---|
| Standard transmission | 5-speed manual | Standard transmission | 5-speed manual |
| Optional transmission | 4-speed automatic | Optional transmission | 4-speed automatic |
| Standard differential ratio | 3.08 | Standard differential ratio | 3.08 |

**Chassis and Suspension**

| | 1987 GT 5.0 | | 1994 GT 5.0 |
|---|---|---|---|
| Frame type | Unit body | Frame type | Unit body |
| Brake type | Power disc/drum | Brake type | Power disc/disc |
| Front suspension | Modified MacPherson strut, lower A-arm, coil springs | Front suspension | Modified MacPherson strut, lower A-arm, coil springs |
| Rear suspension | Live axle, upper and lower trailing arms, coil springs, tube shocks, anti-tramp bars | Rear suspension | Live axle, upper and lower trailing arms, coil springs, tube shocks, anti-tramp bars |
| Steering type | Rack and pinion | Steering type | Rack and pinion |
| Turns (lock to lock) | 3.1 | Turns (lock to lock) | 2.5 |
| Turning circle (ft) | 37.1 | Turning circle (ft) | 38.3 |

**Performance**

| | 1987 GT 5.0 | | 1994 GT 5.0 |
|---|---|---|---|
| 0–30 mph (sec) | 2.3 | 0–30 mph (sec) | 2.4 |
| 0–60 mph (sec) | 6.7 | 0–60 mph (sec) | 6.7 |
| 0–100 mph (sec) | 18.8 | 0–100 mph (sec) | 18.8 est. |
| Standing 1/4 mile (sec) | 15.3 | Standing 1/4 mile (sec) | 15.2 |
| Data source | *Road & Track* | Data source | *Road & Track* |

| Year/Model | 1996 GT 4.6 |
| --- | --- |
| MSRP | $17,610 base, $19,825 as tested |

### Dimensions
| | |
| --- | --- |
| Overall length (in) | 181.5 |
| Wheelbase (in) | 101.3 |
| Width (in) | 71.8 |
| Height (in) | 53.4 |
| Track (in, f/r) | 60.1/58.7 |
| Curb weight (lbs) | 3,580 |

### Engine
| | |
| --- | --- |
| No. of cylinders | 8 |
| Layout | 90 degree V-8, single overhead camshafts, 2 valves per cylinder |
| Construction | Iron block and heads |
| Bore x stroke (mm) | 90.2x90.0 |
| Displacement (cc/ci) | 4,601/281.0 |
| Compression ratio: | 9.0:1 |
| Horsepower rating @ rpm | 215 @ 4,400 |
| Torque rating @ rpm (lb-ft) | 285 @ 3,500 |
| Intake/carburetion | Direct port electronic fuel injection |

### Drivetrain
| | |
| --- | --- |
| Standard transmission | 5-speed manual |
| Optional transmission | 4-speed automatic |
| Standard differential ratio | 3.08 |

### Chassis and Suspension
| | |
| --- | --- |
| Frame type | Unit body |
| Brake type | Power disc/disc |
| Front suspension | Modified MacPherson strut, lower A-arm, coil springs |
| Rear suspension | Live axle, upper and lower trailing arms, coil springs, tube shocks, anti-tramp bars |
| Steering type | Rack and pinion |
| Turns (lock to lock) | 2.4 |
| Turning circle (ft) | 38.3 |

### Performance
| | |
| --- | --- |
| 0–30 mph (sec) | 2.2 |
| 0–60 mph (sec) | 6.8 |
| 0–100 mph (sec) | 18.8 est. |
| Standing 1/4 mile (sec) | 15.3 |
| Data source | Road & Track |

| Year/Model | 1996 SVT Cobra 4.6 convertible |
| --- | --- |
| MSRP | $28,135 base, $30,095 as tested |

### Dimensions
| | |
| --- | --- |
| Overall length (in) | 181.5 |
| Wheelbase (in) | 101.3 |
| Width (in) | 71.8 |
| Height (in) | 53.4 |
| Track (in, f/r) | 60.1/58.7 |
| Curb weight (lbs) | 3,446 |

### Engine
| | |
| --- | --- |
| No. of cylinders | 8 |
| Layout | 90-degree V-8, double overhead camshafts, 4 valves per cylinder |
| Construction | Aluminum-alloy block and heads |
| Bore x stroke (mm) | 90.2x90.0 |
| Displacement (cc/ci) | 4,601/281.0 |
| Compression ratio | 9.9:1 |
| Horsepower rating @ rpm | 305 @ 5,800 |
| Torque rating @ rpm (lb-ft) | 300 @ 4,800 |
| Intake/carburetion | Direct-port electronic fuel injection |

### Drivetrain
| | |
| --- | --- |
| Standard transmission | 5-speed manual |
| Optional transmission | NA |
| Standard differential ratio | 3.27 |

### Chassis and Suspension
| | |
| --- | --- |
| Frame type | Unit body |
| Brake type | Power disc/disc |
| Front suspension | Modified MacPherson strut, lower A-arm, coil springs |
| Rear suspension | Live axle, upper and lower trailing arms, coil springs, tube shocks, anti-tramp bars |
| Steering type | Rack and pinion |
| Turns (lock to lock) | 2.4 |
| Turning circle (ft) | 38.3 |

### Performance
| | |
| --- | --- |
| 0–30 mph (sec) | 2.3 |
| 0–60 mph (sec) | 5.8 |
| 0–100 mph (sec) | 14.2 |
| Standing 1/4 mile (sec) | 14.3 |
| Data source | Road & Track Specials |

# INDEX